Zodiacal Herbage

Zodiacal Herbage

Astrological Insights

Matthew Petchinsky

Apophis Enterprises LLC

Zodiacal Herbage: Astrological Insights: Cannabis Universe: Volume 2

By: Matthew Petchinsky

| 2 |

Part I: The Planets and Their Influence

Introduction to Astrological Insights and Cannabis Universe
Overview of the Book's Goals

Welcome to "Zodiacal Herbage: Astrological Insights: Cannabis Universe: Volume 2." This book is designed to be a comprehensive guide that bridges the ancient wisdom of astrology with the healing and transformative properties of cannabis. Our goals are multifaceted, aiming to provide readers with a deeper understanding of both astrology and cannabis, and how their combined influences can enhance well-being, personal growth, and spiritual awareness.

Key Goals of This Book:

1. **Educate:** To provide a thorough understanding of the twelve zodiac signs, nine planets, celestial bodies, moon phases, and celestial events, and their corresponding influences on individuals and the environment.
2. **Integrate:** To show how specific cannabis strains can complement and enhance the energies and traits associated with each astrological element.
3. **Empower:** To empower readers with the knowledge to use astrology and cannabis intentionally for personal growth, healing, and transformation.
4. **Guide:** To offer practical advice and guidance on selecting and using cannabis strains that align with one's astrological profile and current celestial influences.

The Connection Between Astrology and Cannabis

Astrology, with its roots in ancient civilizations, has long been used as a tool for understanding the self, predicting future events, and navigating life's challenges. It is based on the belief that the positions and movements of celestial bodies (the Sun, Moon, planets, and stars) influence human affairs and natural phenomena.

Cannabis, on the other hand, has been utilized for thousands of years for its medicinal, recreational, and spiritual properties. Its diverse range of strains, each with unique chemical compositions and effects, offers a multitude of benefits, from pain relief and relaxation to enhanced creativity and spiritual awakening.

How Astrology and Cannabis Intersect:

- **Energy Alignment:** Both astrology and cannabis are about harnessing natural energies. Astrology helps us understand the cosmic energies at play, while cannabis allows us to align our physical and mental state with these energies.
- **Personalization:** Just as each person's astrological chart is unique, so too is their response to different cannabis strains. By understanding one's astrological profile, individuals can select strains that best suit their needs and current cosmic conditions.
- **Holistic Healing:** Combining astrology and cannabis promotes holistic healing. Astrology provides insights into emotional and psychological patterns, while cannabis offers physical and mental relief, creating a comprehensive approach to wellness.
- **Mindfulness and Intention:** Using cannabis with astrological knowledge fosters mindfulness and intention. This book encourages readers to use cannabis not just for recreational purposes but as a tool for intentional living and personal growth.

The Importance of Understanding Celestial Influences

Understanding celestial influences is crucial for anyone seeking to live in harmony with the natural rhythms of the universe. Astrology offers a profound framework for interpreting these influences, allowing individuals to make informed decisions, anticipate challenges, and capitalize on opportunities.

Why Celestial Influences Matter:

1. **Self-Awareness:** Knowing how celestial bodies influence your personality, emotions, and behaviors can lead to greater self-awareness and self-acceptance.

2. **Timing:** Astrology can guide you on the best times for various activities, such as starting a new project, making significant life changes, or focusing on self-care.

3. **Growth and Transformation:** By aligning with the natural cycles of the cosmos, you can facilitate personal growth and transformation, navigating life's ups and downs with greater ease and resilience.

4. **Connection:** Understanding celestial influences fosters a deeper connection to the universe and the natural world, reminding us that we are part of a larger, interconnected system.

In "Zodiacal Herbage: Astrological Insights: Cannabis Universe: Volume 2," we will delve into the specific roles of the planets, zodiac signs, celestial bodies, and cosmic events, exploring how these elements shape our experiences and how the right cannabis strains can enhance our journey through the astrological landscape. This integration of ancient wisdom and modern science aims to provide you with a unique, enriched perspective on both astrology and cannabis, empowering

Chapter 1: The Sun: Vitality and Expression
The Sun's Role in Astrology

In astrology, the Sun is one of the most significant celestial bodies, symbolizing the core essence of who we are. It represents our identity, vitality, and the fundamental drive that propels us through life. Often referred to as the "heart" of our astrological chart, the Sun signifies our conscious mind, willpower, and the creative force within us.

Key Aspects of the Sun in Astrology:

1. **Identity and Ego:** The Sun is associated with our sense of self and our ego. It defines how we see ourselves and how we wish to be seen by others. The Sun's position in our birth chart reveals our primary traits and the core of our personality.

2. **Vitality and Energy:** The Sun represents our life force and vitality. Its placement can indicate the source of our energy and how we recharge ourselves. It governs our physical health and overall well-being.

3. **Purpose and Drive:** The Sun guides our ambitions and the path we pursue in life. It highlights our purpose, what motivates us, and the goals we strive to achieve.

4. **Expression and Creativity:** The Sun influences our creative abilities and how we express ourselves. It encourages us to shine and share our unique gifts with the world.

5. **Leadership and Authority:** The Sun also embodies leadership and authority. It signifies the potential for leadership roles and how we assert our influence in various aspects of life.

The Sun's Placement in the Zodiac:

- **Aries Sun:** Dynamic, courageous, and pioneering. Individuals with the Sun in Aries are often natural leaders, full of energy and enthusiasm.
- **Taurus Sun:** Reliable, practical, and grounded. Those with the Sun in Taurus value stability and comfort, often excelling in matters related to the senses and material wealth.
- **Gemini Sun:** Curious, adaptable, and communicative. Gemini Suns are known for their intellectual versatility and social skills.
- **Cancer Sun:** Nurturing, sensitive, and intuitive. The Sun in Cancer emphasizes emotional depth and a strong connection to home and family.
- **Leo Sun:** Charismatic, creative, and confident. Leos, ruled by the Sun, naturally draw attention and are often found in the spotlight.
- **Virgo Sun:** Analytical, meticulous, and service-oriented. Virgos with the Sun exhibit a strong desire to help others and improve their surroundings.
- **Libra Sun:** Diplomatic, balanced, and harmonious. The Sun in Libra highlights a strong sense of justice and a desire for peaceful relationships.
- **Scorpio Sun:** Intense, transformative, and secretive. Scorpio Suns are deeply emotional and often experience life with great intensity.
- **Sagittarius Sun:** Adventurous, optimistic, and philosophical. Individuals with the Sun in Sagittarius are known for their love of exploration and learning.
- **Capricorn Sun:** Ambitious, disciplined, and determined. The Sun in Capricorn emphasizes a strong work ethic and a desire for achievement.

- **Aquarius Sun:** Innovative, independent, and humanitarian. Aquarians with the Sun are forward-thinking and often involved in progressive causes.
- **Pisces Sun:** Compassionate, artistic, and intuitive. Pisces Suns are deeply connected to their emotions and often express themselves through creative outlets.

Cannabis Strains for Enhancing Vitality

Just as the Sun is a source of energy and vitality in astrology, certain cannabis strains can enhance these qualities within us. These strains are selected for their ability to boost energy, promote creativity, and foster a sense of well-being, aligning with the vibrant and expressive nature of the Sun.

Sour Diesel: Energizing and Uplifting

Sour Diesel is a sativa-dominant strain renowned for its fast-acting, energizing effects. It is a popular choice for those seeking to enhance vitality and mental clarity.

- **Effects:** Sour Diesel provides an uplifting and euphoric high, making it ideal for combating fatigue and promoting a positive mindset. It can help spark creativity and motivation, aligning well with the Sun's influence on expression and purpose.
- **Flavor and Aroma:** This strain has a pungent diesel-like aroma with hints of citrus and earthiness, adding to its invigorating profile.
- **Usage:** Sour Diesel is suitable for daytime use, helping individuals stay active, focused, and inspired throughout the day.

Jack Herer: Creative and Euphoric

Named after the famous cannabis activist, Jack Herer is a well-balanced hybrid strain known for its potent, clear-headed effects and ability to enhance creativity and concentration.

- **Effects:** Jack Herer offers a blissful, euphoric high that stimulates both the mind and body. It promotes a sense of well-being and encourages creative thinking, making it a perfect complement to the Sun's role in fostering expression and vitality.
- **Flavor and Aroma:** The strain has a distinctive aroma with notes of pine, earth, and citrus, contributing to its refreshing and energizing effects.
- **Usage:** Jack Herer is often used during creative endeavors or social activities, providing a burst of energy and inspiration without overwhelming the senses.

Green Crack: Focused and Motivating

Green Crack, despite its controversial name, is a pure sativa strain famous for its sharp, invigorating effects. It is ideal for those needing a substantial energy boost and mental clarity.

- **Effects:** Green Crack delivers a potent cerebral high that enhances focus, energy, and motivation. Its effects are long-lasting and can help combat stress and fatigue, aligning perfectly with the Sun's attributes of vitality and drive.
- **Flavor and Aroma:** This strain has a tangy, fruity flavor reminiscent of mango, with an earthy undertone that adds to its vibrant profile.
- **Usage:** Green Crack is best used during the day when mental alertness and physical activity are required, helping individuals tackle tasks with enthusiasm and vigor.

Pineapple Express: Balanced and Euphoric

Pineapple Express is a hybrid strain known for its balanced effects, offering both mental stimulation and physical relaxation. It is a favorite for those seeking a harmonious blend of energy and calmness.

- **Effects:** Pineapple Express provides a mild, euphoric high that promotes happiness and creativity. It enhances focus and productivity while also offering a subtle body relaxation, making it a versatile strain that resonates with the Sun's attributes of vitality and expression.
- **Flavor and Aroma:** This strain has a delightful tropical aroma with hints of pineapple and citrus, contributing to its refreshing and enjoyable effects.
- **Usage:** Pineapple Express is suitable for any time of day, particularly when a balanced approach to energy and relaxation is desired.

Durban Poison: Pure Energy and Focus

Durban Poison is a pure sativa strain originating from South Africa, known for its invigorating and uplifting effects. It is perfect for those seeking a natural boost in energy and mental clarity.

- **Effects:** Durban Poison delivers a strong, cerebral high that enhances focus, creativity, and productivity. It is a go-to strain for daytime activities and creative projects, aligning well with the Sun's influence on vitality and expression.
- **Flavor and Aroma:** This strain has a sweet, earthy aroma with a hint of pine, adding to its energizing properties.
- **Usage:** Durban Poison is ideal for daytime use, providing a sustained boost in energy and mental sharpness, helping individuals stay active and engaged.

Conclusion

In astrology, the Sun is the source of our vitality, expression, and core identity. Understanding its role can help us align with our true selves and harness our innate strengths. By integrating specific cannabis strains that enhance vitality and creativity, such as Sour Diesel, Jack Herer, Green Crack, Pineapple Express, and Durban Poison, we can further amplify the positive influences of the Sun in our lives. These strains offer a natural way to boost energy, enhance creativity, and promote a sense of well-being, helping us to shine brightly and express our true essence, just as the Sun does in the cosmos.

Check out my Virtual dispensary for all your hemp needs: https://shift.store/sg1fan23477/retail

Chapter 2: The Moon: Emotions and Intuition
The Moon's Influence on Emotions and Intuition

In astrology, the Moon is the celestial body that governs our emotions, intuition, and inner world. It represents the subconscious mind, our instinctive reactions, and the way we process our feelings. The Moon is closely linked to our sense of security, nurturing, and how we respond to life's experiences on an emotional level.

Key Aspects of the Moon in Astrology:

1. **Emotions and Feelings:** The Moon symbolizes our deepest emotions and how we express them. It reflects our emotional responses and needs, influencing how we handle relationships and our emotional well-being.

2. **Intuition and Subconscious:** The Moon is associated with intuition and the subconscious mind. It guides our gut feelings and instincts, often revealing truths that our conscious mind may not readily acknowledge.

3. **Nurturing and Comfort:** The Moon represents the nurturing aspect of our personality. It influences how we give and receive care, seek comfort, and create a sense of home and belonging.

4. **Cycles and Rhythms:** The Moon's phases reflect the natural cycles and rhythms of life. These cycles influence our moods, behaviors, and how we navigate through different periods of growth and change.

5. **Memory and Past:** The Moon also relates to our memories and connection to the past. It holds the key to our emotional history and how it shapes our present and future.

The Moon's Placement in the Zodiac:

- **Aries Moon:** Quick-tempered, assertive, and passionate. Aries Moons feel emotions intensely and express them directly.
- **Taurus Moon:** Stable, practical, and comfort-seeking. Taurus Moons value security and are emotionally resilient.
- **Gemini Moon:** Curious, communicative, and adaptable. Gemini Moons are emotionally versatile and intellectually stimulated.
- **Cancer Moon:** Nurturing, sensitive, and intuitive. Cancer Moons are deeply connected to their emotions and family.
- **Leo Moon:** Dramatic, expressive, and affectionate. Leo Moons enjoy being the center of attention and seek validation.
- **Virgo Moon:** Analytical, practical, and detail-oriented. Virgo Moons approach emotions with logic and a desire to help.
- **Libra Moon:** Diplomatic, balanced, and harmonious. Libra Moons seek emotional balance and harmonious relationships.
- **Scorpio Moon:** Intense, secretive, and transformative. Scorpio Moons experience emotions deeply and are often introspective.
- **Sagittarius Moon:** Optimistic, adventurous, and philosophical. Sagittarius Moons are emotionally expansive and seek freedom.
- **Capricorn Moon:** Reserved, disciplined, and ambitious. Capricorn Moons are emotionally controlled and focused on goals.
- **Aquarius Moon:** Detached, innovative, and humanitarian. Aquarius Moons approach emotions intellectually and seek social connections.
- **Pisces Moon:** Compassionate, empathetic, and dreamy. Pisces Moons are highly intuitive and emotionally sensitive.

Cannabis Strains for Emotional Balance

The Moon's influence on our emotions and intuition makes it essential to find ways to maintain emotional balance and inner peace. Certain cannabis strains can help stabilize moods, reduce stress, and enhance emotional well-being, aligning with the nurturing and intuitive qualities of the Moon.

Blue Dream: Calming and Uplifting

Blue Dream is a hybrid strain renowned for its balanced effects that provide both relaxation and mental invigoration. It is an excellent choice for those seeking emotional balance and stress relief.

- **Effects:** Blue Dream offers a gentle, euphoric high that helps to calm the mind and uplift the spirit. It provides a sense of mental clarity and relaxation without sedation, making it ideal for managing stress and anxiety.
- **Flavor and Aroma:** This strain has a sweet, berry-like aroma with earthy undertones, contributing to its soothing effects.
- **Usage:** Blue Dream is suitable for any time of day, providing emotional stability and a positive mindset without overwhelming the senses.

Northern Lights: Relaxing and Soothing

Northern Lights is a classic indica strain known for its deeply relaxing and calming effects. It is highly effective for those needing to unwind and achieve emotional tranquility.

- **Effects:** Northern Lights delivers a potent, body-focused high that promotes relaxation and sleep. Its calming effects help to alleviate stress, anxiety, and emotional tension, making it a perfect strain for nighttime use.
- **Flavor and Aroma:** This strain has a sweet, earthy aroma with hints of pine and spice, adding to its comforting profile.
- **Usage:** Northern Lights is best used in the evening or before bed to help relax the body and mind, promoting restful sleep and emotional peace.

Lavender: Tranquil and Sedative

Lavender is an indica-dominant strain known for its strong calming and sedative effects. It is ideal for those seeking deep relaxation and emotional relief.

- **Effects:** Lavender provides a heavy, tranquilizing high that eases the mind and body into a state of deep relaxation. It is effective for reducing stress, anxiety, and emotional turmoil, helping users find peace and comfort.
- **Flavor and Aroma:** This strain has a floral, lavender-like aroma with hints of herbs and spices, enhancing its soothing properties.
- **Usage:** Lavender is best used in the evening or during periods of high stress to promote emotional balance and restful sleep.

Granddaddy Purple: Stress Relief and Relaxation

Granddaddy Purple is a popular indica strain known for its powerful relaxing effects and ability to alleviate stress and anxiety.

- **Effects:** Granddaddy Purple offers a calming, euphoric high that helps to reduce stress and promote relaxation. Its soothing effects make it an excellent choice for managing emotional imbalances and promoting a sense of well-being.
- **Flavor and Aroma:** This strain has a sweet, grape-like aroma with earthy undertones, adding to its relaxing effects.
- **Usage:** Granddaddy Purple is best used in the evening to help unwind and relax after a stressful day, providing emotional comfort and peace.

Amnesia Haze: Energizing and Mood-Enhancing

Amnesia Haze is a sativa-dominant strain known for its uplifting and mood-enhancing effects. It is perfect for those needing an emotional boost and mental clarity.

- **Effects:** Amnesia Haze delivers a cerebral, euphoric high that enhances mood and energy levels. It helps to reduce stress and anxiety while promoting a positive, optimistic outlook.
- **Flavor and Aroma:** This strain has a citrusy, earthy aroma with hints of sweetness, contributing to its energizing effects.
- **Usage:** Amnesia Haze is suitable for daytime use, providing a boost in energy and mood without causing sedation.

Conclusion

The Moon in astrology governs our emotions, intuition, and inner world. Understanding its influence can help us navigate our emotional landscape with greater awareness and balance. By integrating specific cannabis strains that promote emotional balance and relaxation, such as Blue Dream, Northern Lights, Lavender, Granddaddy Purple, and Amnesia Haze, we can enhance our ability to manage stress, find inner peace, and connect with our intuitive selves. These strains offer a natural way to stabilize moods, reduce anxiety, and promote overall emotional well-being, aligning us with the nurturing and intuitive qualities of the Moon.

Check out my Virtual dispensary for all your hemp needs: https://shift.store/sg1fan23477/retail

Chapter 3: Mercury: Communication and Intellect

Mercury's Impact on Communication and Intellect

In astrology, Mercury is the planet that governs communication, intellect, and the way we process information. Named after the Roman messenger god, Mercury is associated with how we think, express ourselves, and interact with the world around us. It influences our mental agility, speech, writing, and all forms of communication.

Key Aspects of Mercury in Astrology:

1. **Communication:** Mercury rules all forms of communication, including speaking, writing, and non-verbal expression. Its position in our birth chart reveals how we convey ideas and connect with others.

2. **Intellect and Reasoning:** Mercury governs our intellect, logical reasoning, and analytical skills. It influences our ability to learn, think critically, and solve problems.

3. **Curiosity and Learning:** This planet drives our curiosity and desire for knowledge. It motivates us to explore, ask questions, and seek understanding.

4. **Adaptability:** Mercury is known for its adaptability and versatility. It helps us adjust to new situations, think on our feet, and navigate changes with ease.

5. **Commerce and Travel:** Historically, Mercury also represents commerce, trade, and travel. It influences our negotiation skills, business acumen, and how we move through the world.

Mercury's Placement in the Zodiac:

- **Aries Mercury:** Direct, quick-thinking, and assertive. Aries Mercury individuals communicate with confidence and enthusiasm.
- **Taurus Mercury:** Practical, deliberate, and reliable. Taurus Mercury individuals prefer clear, straightforward communication and have a methodical approach to learning.
- **Gemini Mercury:** Versatile, curious, and sociable. Gemini Mercury individuals excel in communication, quick thinking, and adaptability.
- **Cancer Mercury:** Intuitive, emotional, and reflective. Cancer Mercury individuals communicate with empathy and sensitivity, often relying on their intuition.
- **Leo Mercury:** Dramatic, expressive, and confident. Leo Mercury individuals communicate with flair and creativity, often captivating their audience.
- **Virgo Mercury:** Analytical, precise, and detail-oriented. Virgo Mercury individuals are excellent at critical thinking, organization, and clear communication.
- **Libra Mercury:** Diplomatic, fair-minded, and sociable. Libra Mercury individuals excel in balanced communication, mediation, and social interactions.
- **Scorpio Mercury:** Intense, probing, and secretive. Scorpio Mercury individuals communicate with depth and intensity, often seeking hidden truths.
- **Sagittarius Mercury:** Philosophical, optimistic, and expansive. Sagittarius Mercury individuals are open-minded, love learning, and enjoy sharing their insights.
- **Capricorn Mercury:** Practical, disciplined, and strategic. Capricorn Mercury individuals communicate with purpose and structure, focusing on goals and achievements.
- **Aquarius Mercury:** Innovative, independent, and humanitarian. Aquarius Mercury individuals are forward-thinking, often communicating unconventional ideas.

- **Pisces Mercury:** Imaginative, intuitive, and compassionate. Pisces Mercury individuals communicate with creativity and empathy, often blending reality with fantasy.

Cannabis Strains for Mental Clarity

Mercury's influence on communication and intellect makes it essential to maintain mental clarity and cognitive function. Certain cannabis strains can enhance focus, improve cognitive abilities, and promote clear thinking, aligning with the quick-witted and analytical nature of Mercury.

Harlequin: Clear-Headed and Focused

Harlequin is a sativa-dominant strain known for its high CBD content and clear-headed effects. It is an excellent choice for those seeking mental clarity without intense psychoactive effects.

- **Effects:** Harlequin offers a balanced, clear-headed high that enhances focus and concentration. Its high CBD content helps to reduce anxiety and promote mental calmness, making it ideal for tasks requiring precision and clear thinking.
- **Flavor and Aroma:** This strain has an earthy, woody aroma with hints of mango and citrus, contributing to its refreshing profile.
- **Usage:** Harlequin is suitable for daytime use, providing mental clarity and focus without overwhelming psychoactive effects.

ACDC: Non-Psychoactive and Relaxing

ACDC is a hybrid strain renowned for its high CBD content and minimal psychoactive effects. It is perfect for those seeking relaxation and mental clarity without the high.

- **Effects:** ACDC provides a relaxing, clear-headed high that enhances focus and reduces stress. Its high CBD content helps to calm the mind and body, making it suitable for tasks requiring mental clarity and composure.

- **Flavor and Aroma:** This strain has a sweet, earthy aroma with hints of citrus and pine, adding to its calming effects.
- **Usage:** ACDC is best used during the day when mental alertness and relaxation are needed, providing a clear mind and calm demeanor.

Sour Tsunami: Balanced and Clear-Headed

Sour Tsunami is a hybrid strain known for its high CBD content and balanced effects. It is ideal for those seeking clear-headedness and relaxation.

- **Effects:** Sour Tsunami offers a balanced high that enhances focus and mental clarity. Its high CBD content helps to reduce stress and anxiety, promoting a calm and clear mind.
- **Flavor and Aroma:** This strain has a sour, earthy aroma with hints of citrus and diesel, contributing to its invigorating profile.
- **Usage:** Sour Tsunami is suitable for any time of day, providing mental clarity and relaxation without intense psychoactive effects.

Cannatonic: Relaxing and Uplifting

Cannatonic is a hybrid strain known for its balanced THC and CBD content, providing mild psychoactive effects and clear-headed relaxation.

- **Effects:** Cannatonic offers a relaxing, uplifting high that promotes mental clarity and focus. Its balanced THC and CBD content helps to reduce stress and enhance cognitive function without overwhelming euphoria.
- **Flavor and Aroma:** This strain has a mild, earthy aroma with hints of pine and citrus, contributing to its soothing effects.
- **Usage:** Cannatonic is suitable for daytime use, providing a balanced approach to relaxation and mental clarity.

Canna-Tsu: Focused and Clear-Headed

Canna-Tsu is a hybrid strain known for its high CBD content and minimal psychoactive effects. It is perfect for those seeking mental clarity and focus.

- **Effects:** Canna-Tsu provides a clear-headed, focused high that enhances cognitive function and reduces stress. Its high CBD content helps to calm the mind and promote mental clarity without intense psychoactive effects.
- **Flavor and Aroma:** This strain has an earthy, citrus aroma with hints of sweetness, adding to its refreshing profile.
- **Usage:** Canna-Tsu is best used during the day when mental alertness and relaxation are needed, providing a clear mind and focused demeanor.

Conclusion

Mercury in astrology governs our communication, intellect, and the way we process information. Understanding its influence can help us enhance our cognitive abilities, improve communication, and maintain mental clarity. By integrating specific cannabis strains that promote mental clarity and focus, such as Harlequin, ACDC, Sour Tsunami, Cannatonic, and Canna-Tsu, we can enhance our ability to think clearly, communicate effectively, and navigate the complexities of life with ease. These strains offer a natural way to boost cognitive function, reduce anxiety, and promote overall mental well-being, aligning us with the quick-witted and analytical qualities of Mercury.

Check out my Virtual dispensary for all your hemp needs: https://shift.store/sg1fan23477/retail

Chapter 4: Venus: Love and Beauty

Venus's Influence on Relationships and Aesthetics

In astrology, Venus is the planet that governs love, beauty, and harmony. Named after the Roman goddess of love, Venus influences our romantic relationships, our sense of aesthetics, and our appreciation of the finer things in life. It represents how we express affection, what we find beautiful, and how we create and maintain balance in our interactions.

Key Aspects of Venus in Astrology:

1. **Love and Relationships:** Venus rules over romantic love, partnerships, and our capacity for affection. Its placement in our birth chart reveals how we approach relationships, our needs in love, and the qualities we seek in partners.

2. **Aesthetics and Beauty:** Venus influences our sense of beauty, art, and aesthetics. It governs our taste in fashion, decor, and all forms of artistic expression, highlighting what we find visually appealing.

3. **Harmony and Balance:** Venus promotes harmony, balance, and cooperation in our interactions. It helps us navigate social dynamics, fostering peace and understanding in relationships.

4. **Pleasure and Enjoyment:** Venus is associated with pleasure, indulgence, and the enjoyment of life's sensory experiences. It highlights our desires for comfort, luxury, and the good things in life.

5. **Values and Desires:** Venus also represents our values and what we desire most. It guides our choices, from romantic partners to material possessions, reflecting what we value and cherish.

Venus's Placement in the Zodiac:

- **Aries Venus:** Passionate, impulsive, and adventurous. Aries Venus individuals seek excitement and spontaneity in love.
- **Taurus Venus:** Loyal, sensual, and grounded. Taurus Venus individuals value stability and comfort, enjoying the pleasures of the senses.
- **Gemini Venus:** Playful, communicative, and curious. Gemini Venus individuals thrive on intellectual stimulation and variety in relationships.
- **Cancer Venus:** Nurturing, sensitive, and emotional. Cancer Venus individuals seek deep emotional connections and a sense of security in love.
- **Leo Venus:** Charismatic, generous, and dramatic. Leo Venus individuals enjoy being admired and appreciated, often expressing love grandly.
- **Virgo Venus:** Practical, attentive, and detail-oriented. Virgo Venus individuals show love through acts of service and attention to detail.
- **Libra Venus:** Diplomatic, charming, and balanced. Libra Venus individuals value harmony and equality in relationships, often seeking beauty and balance.
- **Scorpio Venus:** Intense, passionate, and transformative. Scorpio Venus individuals desire deep, transformative connections in love.
- **Sagittarius Venus:** Free-spirited, adventurous, and philosophical. Sagittarius Venus individuals seek freedom and growth in relationships, valuing honesty and exploration.
- **Capricorn Venus:** Reserved, ambitious, and disciplined. Capricorn Venus individuals approach love with seriousness and a desire for long-term commitment.
- **Aquarius Venus:** Unconventional, independent, and progressive. Aquarius Venus individuals value individuality and intellectual connections in love.

- **Pisces Venus:** Romantic, empathetic, and dreamy. Pisces Venus individuals seek soulful, compassionate connections, often idealizing love.

Cannabis Strains for Enhancing Love and Beauty

Venus's influence on love and beauty makes it essential to find ways to enhance these aspects in our lives. Certain cannabis strains can amplify feelings of affection, promote relaxation, and enhance our appreciation of aesthetics, aligning with the harmonious and pleasurable nature of Venus.

Strawberry Cough: Uplifting and Euphoric

Strawberry Cough is a sativa-dominant strain known for its uplifting and euphoric effects. It is an excellent choice for enhancing mood and promoting a positive atmosphere.

- **Effects:** Strawberry Cough offers a cerebral, uplifting high that promotes feelings of happiness and well-being. Its euphoric effects can enhance social interactions and create a loving, relaxed environment.
- **Flavor and Aroma:** This strain has a sweet, strawberry-like aroma with hints of spice, adding to its delightful sensory experience.
- **Usage:** Strawberry Cough is suitable for daytime use, providing a boost in mood and energy that enhances social and romantic interactions.

Cherry Pie: Relaxing and Blissful

Cherry Pie is a hybrid strain known for its balanced effects and sweet, fruity flavor. It is perfect for those seeking relaxation and a sense of well-being.

- **Effects:** Cherry Pie offers a calming, blissful high that helps to reduce stress and promote relaxation. Its balanced effects make it ideal for enhancing feelings of love and connection, fostering a warm and affectionate atmosphere.

- **Flavor and Aroma:** This strain has a sweet, cherry-like aroma with earthy undertones, contributing to its soothing and enjoyable experience.
- **Usage:** Cherry Pie is suitable for any time of day, providing relaxation and a positive mood that enhances romantic and social interactions.

Pink Kush: Calming and Sedative

Pink Kush is an indica-dominant strain known for its potent relaxing effects and sweet, floral aroma. It is ideal for those seeking deep relaxation and a sense of tranquility.

- **Effects:** Pink Kush provides a heavy, calming high that promotes deep relaxation and stress relief. Its sedative effects can enhance feelings of intimacy and comfort, making it perfect for romantic evenings.
- **Flavor and Aroma:** This strain has a sweet, floral aroma with hints of vanilla and candy, adding to its luxurious and indulgent experience.
- **Usage:** Pink Kush is best used in the evening or before bed to promote relaxation and enhance romantic connections.

Lavender: Tranquil and Soothing

Lavender is an indica-dominant strain known for its strong calming and sedative effects. It is ideal for those seeking deep relaxation and emotional relief.

- **Effects:** Lavender provides a heavy, tranquilizing high that eases the mind and body into a state of deep relaxation. It is effective for reducing stress and promoting a calm, intimate atmosphere, making it perfect for romantic moments.

- **Flavor and Aroma:** This strain has a floral, lavender-like aroma with hints of herbs and spices, enhancing its soothing properties.
- **Usage:** Lavender is best used in the evening or during periods of high stress to promote emotional balance and restful sleep.

Blueberry: Euphoric and Relaxing

Blueberry is an indica-dominant strain known for its relaxing and euphoric effects. It is perfect for those seeking a sense of well-being and relaxation.

- **Effects:** Blueberry offers a calming, euphoric high that promotes relaxation and happiness. Its soothing effects can enhance feelings of love and connection, making it ideal for intimate moments.
- **Flavor and Aroma:** This strain has a sweet, berry-like aroma with earthy undertones, adding to its delightful sensory experience.
- **Usage:** Blueberry is suitable for any time of day, providing relaxation and a positive mood that enhances romantic and social interactions.

Conclusion

Venus in astrology governs our sense of love, beauty, and harmony. Understanding its influence can help us enhance our relationships, appreciate beauty, and create a balanced, enjoyable life. By integrating specific cannabis strains that promote feelings of love, relaxation, and aesthetic appreciation, such as Strawberry Cough, Cherry Pie, Pink Kush, Lavender, and Blueberry, we can enhance our ability to connect with others, enjoy life's pleasures, and find beauty in the world around us. These strains offer a natural way to boost mood, reduce stress, and promote overall well-being, aligning us with the harmonious and pleasurable qualities of Venus.

Check out my Virtual dispensary for all your hemp needs: https://shift.store/sg1fan23477/retail

Chapter 5: Mars: Energy and Action
Mars's Role in Driving Energy and Action

In astrology, Mars is the planet that governs energy, action, and desire. Named after the Roman god of war, Mars influences our drive, determination, and the way we assert ourselves in the world. It represents our physical vitality, courage, and the impulses that propel us to take action and pursue our goals.

Key Aspects of Mars in Astrology:

1. **Energy and Vitality:** Mars symbolizes our physical energy and stamina. It influences how we exert ourselves, our endurance, and our overall vitality.
2. **Action and Initiative:** Mars drives our ability to take action and initiative. It represents our assertiveness, how we handle challenges, and our capacity to act decisively.
3. **Desire and Passion:** Mars governs our desires and passions, including our sexual energy. It reflects what motivates us and what we are passionate about.
4. **Aggression and Conflict:** Mars also represents aggression and conflict. It shows how we express anger, compete, and confront obstacles.
5. **Courage and Strength:** Mars embodies courage and physical strength. It influences our bravery and willingness to face challenges head-on.

Mars's Placement in the Zodiac:

- **Aries Mars:** Energetic, bold, and pioneering. Aries Mars individuals are natural leaders, driven by a desire to initiate and conquer.

- **Taurus Mars:** Persistent, determined, and patient. Taurus Mars individuals have a steady, enduring energy and are motivated by tangible results.
- **Gemini Mars:** Versatile, quick-witted, and curious. Gemini Mars individuals are mentally energetic and thrive on variety and stimulation.
- **Cancer Mars:** Protective, tenacious, and emotional. Cancer Mars individuals channel their energy into nurturing and defending loved ones.
- **Leo Mars:** Confident, ambitious, and dramatic. Leo Mars individuals have a powerful drive to shine and be recognized for their achievements.
- **Virgo Mars:** Analytical, efficient, and meticulous. Virgo Mars individuals are driven by a desire to improve and perfect.
- **Libra Mars:** Diplomatic, strategic, and cooperative. Libra Mars individuals are motivated by harmony and balance, often seeking fair solutions.
- **Scorpio Mars:** Intense, focused, and transformative. Scorpio Mars individuals have a deep, powerful energy that drives them to pursue their passions with determination.
- **Sagittarius Mars:** Adventurous, enthusiastic, and freedom-loving. Sagittarius Mars individuals are driven by a desire for exploration and new experiences.
- **Capricorn Mars:** Ambitious, disciplined, and pragmatic. Capricorn Mars individuals have a strong drive to achieve their long-term goals through hard work and perseverance.
- **Aquarius Mars:** Innovative, independent, and unconventional. Aquarius Mars individuals are motivated by progress and often pursue unique or revolutionary ideas.
- **Pisces Mars:** Compassionate, intuitive, and adaptable. Pisces Mars individuals channel their energy into creative and altruistic pursuits, often guided by their intuition.

Cannabis Strains for Boosting Energy

Mars's influence on energy and action makes it essential to find ways to enhance physical vitality and motivation. Certain cannabis strains can boost energy levels, promote focus, and increase motivation, aligning with the dynamic and assertive nature of Mars.

Durban Poison: Pure Energy and Focus

Durban Poison is a pure sativa strain originating from South Africa, known for its invigorating and uplifting effects. It is perfect for those seeking a natural boost in energy and mental clarity.

- **Effects:** Durban Poison delivers a strong, cerebral high that enhances focus, creativity, and productivity. Its energizing effects help combat fatigue and promote a sense of motivation and enthusiasm, aligning perfectly with Mars's attributes of energy and action.
- **Flavor and Aroma:** This strain has a sweet, earthy aroma with hints of pine and spice, adding to its invigorating profile.
- **Usage:** Durban Poison is ideal for daytime use, providing a sustained boost in energy and mental sharpness, helping individuals stay active and engaged.

Green Crack: Energizing and Motivating

Green Crack, despite its controversial name, is a pure sativa strain famed for its sharp, invigorating effects. It is ideal for those needing a substantial energy boost and mental clarity.

- **Effects:** Green Crack delivers a potent cerebral high that enhances focus, energy, and motivation. Its effects are long-lasting and can help combat stress and fatigue, making it an excellent complement to Mars's drive for action and achievement.
- **Flavor and Aroma:** This strain has a tangy, fruity flavor reminiscent of mango, with an earthy undertone that adds to its vibrant profile.

- **Usage:** Green Crack is best used during the day when mental alertness and physical activity are required, helping individuals tackle tasks with enthusiasm and vigor.

Sour Diesel: Uplifting and Euphoric

Sour Diesel is a sativa-dominant strain renowned for its fast-acting, energizing effects. It is a popular choice for those seeking to enhance vitality and mental clarity.

- **Effects:** Sour Diesel provides an uplifting and euphoric high, making it ideal for combating fatigue and promoting a positive mindset. It can help spark creativity and motivation, aligning well with Mars's influence on energy and action.
- **Flavor and Aroma:** This strain has a pungent diesel-like aroma with hints of citrus and earthiness, adding to its invigorating profile.
- **Usage:** Sour Diesel is suitable for daytime use, helping individuals stay active, focused, and inspired throughout the day.

Jack Herer: Creative and Energizing

Named after the famous cannabis activist, Jack Herer is a well-balanced hybrid strain known for its potent, clear-headed effects and ability to enhance creativity and concentration.

- **Effects:** Jack Herer offers a blissful, euphoric high that stimulates both the mind and body. It promotes a sense of well-being and encourages creative thinking, making it a perfect complement to Mars's role in driving energy and action.
- **Flavor and Aroma:** The strain has a distinctive aroma with notes of pine, earth, and citrus, contributing to its refreshing and energizing effects.

- **Usage:** Jack Herer is often used during creative endeavors or social activities, providing a burst of energy and inspiration without overwhelming the senses.

Super Lemon Haze: Energizing and Uplifting

Super Lemon Haze is a sativa-dominant hybrid known for its lively, uplifting effects and tangy lemon flavor. It is ideal for those seeking an energy boost and enhanced mood.

- **Effects:** Super Lemon Haze provides a cheerful, energetic high that promotes focus, creativity, and motivation. Its uplifting effects help to reduce stress and enhance productivity, aligning with Mars's dynamic and assertive qualities.
- **Flavor and Aroma:** This strain has a zesty, citrusy aroma with sweet undertones, adding to its refreshing and invigorating profile.
- **Usage:** Super Lemon Haze is suitable for daytime use, providing a sustained boost in energy and mood, helping individuals stay active and engaged.

Conclusion

Mars in astrology governs our energy, action, and drive. Understanding its influence can help us harness our physical vitality, take decisive action, and pursue our goals with determination. By integrating specific cannabis strains that boost energy, promote focus, and enhance motivation, such as Durban Poison, Green Crack, Sour Diesel, Jack Herer, and Super Lemon Haze, we can align ourselves with Mars's dynamic and assertive qualities. These strains offer a natural way to increase energy levels, improve mental clarity, and promote overall physical well-being, empowering us to tackle challenges, achieve our goals, and live with vigor and purpose.

Check out my Virtual dispensary for all your hemp needs: https://shift.store/sg1fan23477/retail

Chapter 6: Jupiter: Growth and Expansion
Jupiter's Impact on Growth and Expansion

In astrology, Jupiter is the planet that governs growth, expansion, and abundance. Named after the king of the Roman gods, Jupiter is associated with luck, wisdom, and the pursuit of knowledge. It represents the principles of growth, expansion, and prosperity, influencing our desire for exploration and the broadening of our horizons.

Key Aspects of Jupiter in Astrology:

1. **Growth and Abundance:** Jupiter symbolizes growth, expansion, and abundance in all areas of life. It encourages us to reach beyond our limits and seek greater experiences and knowledge.

2. **Wisdom and Knowledge:** Jupiter governs higher learning, philosophy, and the quest for wisdom. It influences our intellectual pursuits, belief systems, and desire for understanding.

3. **Luck and Optimism:** Jupiter is often associated with good fortune and optimism. Its placement in our birth chart can indicate areas of life where we are likely to experience luck and opportunities.

4. **Travel and Exploration:** Jupiter influences travel and exploration, both physical and intellectual. It drives our desire to explore new territories, cultures, and ideas.

5. **Generosity and Benevolence:** Jupiter embodies generosity, benevolence, and the desire to help others. It encourages us to share our abundance and spread positivity.

Jupiter's Placement in the Zodiac:

- **Aries Jupiter:** Adventurous, bold, and pioneering. Aries Jupiter individuals seek growth through new experiences and taking risks.
- **Taurus Jupiter:** Practical, stable, and sensual. Taurus Jupiter individuals value material growth and seek abundance through practical means.

- **Gemini Jupiter:** Curious, communicative, and versatile. Gemini Jupiter individuals pursue growth through learning and intellectual exploration.
- **Cancer Jupiter:** Nurturing, intuitive, and emotional. Cancer Jupiter individuals seek growth through emotional connections and creating a sense of home.
- **Leo Jupiter:** Confident, generous, and dramatic. Leo Jupiter individuals seek growth through self-expression and creative endeavors.
- **Virgo Jupiter:** Analytical, meticulous, and service-oriented. Virgo Jupiter individuals pursue growth through helping others and improving their environment.
- **Libra Jupiter:** Diplomatic, harmonious, and sociable. Libra Jupiter individuals seek growth through relationships and creating balance in their lives.
- **Scorpio Jupiter:** Intense, transformative, and secretive. Scorpio Jupiter individuals pursue growth through deep emotional and psychological exploration.
- **Sagittarius Jupiter:** Optimistic, adventurous, and philosophical. Sagittarius Jupiter individuals seek growth through travel, learning, and expanding their horizons.
- **Capricorn Jupiter:** Ambitious, disciplined, and pragmatic. Capricorn Jupiter individuals pursue growth through hard work, discipline, and achieving their goals.
- **Aquarius Jupiter:** Innovative, independent, and humanitarian. Aquarius Jupiter individuals seek growth through unconventional ideas and progressive change.
- **Pisces Jupiter:** Compassionate, empathetic, and dreamy. Pisces Jupiter individuals pursue growth through spiritual and creative pursuits.

Cannabis Strains for Growth and Creativity

Jupiter's influence on growth and expansion makes it essential to find ways to enhance creativity and personal development. Certain cannabis strains can boost creativity, inspire new ideas, and promote a sense of well-being, aligning with the expansive and optimistic nature of Jupiter.

Super Lemon Haze: Energizing and Uplifting

Super Lemon Haze is a sativa-dominant hybrid known for its lively, uplifting effects and tangy lemon flavor. It is ideal for those seeking an energy boost and enhanced creativity.

- **Effects:** Super Lemon Haze provides a cheerful, energetic high that promotes focus, creativity, and motivation. Its uplifting effects help to reduce stress and enhance productivity, aligning with Jupiter's expansive and optimistic qualities.
- **Flavor and Aroma:** This strain has a zesty, citrusy aroma with sweet undertones, adding to its refreshing and invigorating profile.
- **Usage:** Super Lemon Haze is suitable for daytime use, providing a sustained boost in energy and mood, helping individuals stay active and engaged.

Blue Dream: Creative and Euphoric

Blue Dream is a hybrid strain celebrated for its balanced effects that provide both relaxation and mental invigoration. It is an excellent choice for those seeking to enhance creativity and stress relief.

- **Effects:** Blue Dream offers a gentle, euphoric high that helps to calm the mind and uplift the spirit. It provides a sense of mental clarity and relaxation without sedation, making it ideal for creative projects and personal growth.
- **Flavor and Aroma:** This strain has a sweet, berry-like aroma with earthy undertones, contributing to its soothing effects.

- **Usage:** Blue Dream is suitable for any time of day, providing emotional stability and a positive mindset without overwhelming the senses.

Sour Tangie: Uplifting and Energizing

Sour Tangie is a sativa-dominant hybrid known for its potent, uplifting effects and tangy citrus flavor. It is perfect for those seeking an energy boost and enhanced mood.

- **Effects:** Sour Tangie delivers a strong, cerebral high that enhances focus, creativity, and motivation. Its energizing effects help combat fatigue and promote a sense of enthusiasm and optimism, aligning with Jupiter's growth-oriented nature.
- **Flavor and Aroma:** This strain has a tangy, citrusy aroma with sweet undertones, adding to its invigorating profile.
- **Usage:** Sour Tangie is ideal for daytime use, providing a sustained boost in energy and mental sharpness, helping individuals stay active and engaged.

Pineapple Express: Balanced and Euphoric

Pineapple Express is a hybrid strain known for its balanced effects, offering both mental stimulation and physical relaxation. It is a favorite for those seeking a harmonious blend of energy and calmness.

- **Effects:** Pineapple Express provides a mild, euphoric high that promotes happiness and creativity. It enhances focus and productivity while also offering a subtle body relaxation, making it a versatile strain that resonates with Jupiter's attributes of growth and expansion.
- **Flavor and Aroma:** This strain has a delightful tropical aroma with hints of pineapple and citrus, contributing to its refreshing and enjoyable effects.

- **Usage:** Pineapple Express is suitable for any time of day, particularly when a balanced approach to energy and relaxation is desired.

Amnesia Haze: Energizing and Mood-Enhancing

Amnesia Haze is a sativa-dominant strain known for its uplifting and mood-enhancing effects. It is perfect for those needing an emotional boost and mental clarity.

- **Effects:** Amnesia Haze delivers a cerebral, euphoric high that enhances mood and energy levels. It helps to reduce stress and anxiety while promoting a positive, optimistic outlook.
- **Flavor and Aroma:** This strain has a citrusy, earthy aroma with hints of sweetness, contributing to its energizing effects.
- **Usage:** Amnesia Haze is suitable for daytime use, providing a boost in energy and mood without causing sedation.

Conclusion

Jupiter in astrology governs our growth, expansion, and pursuit of knowledge. Understanding its influence can help us embrace opportunities for personal development, enhance our creativity, and cultivate a positive outlook on life. By integrating specific cannabis strains that promote growth and creativity, such as Super Lemon Haze, Blue Dream, Sour Tangie, Pineapple Express, and Amnesia Haze, we can enhance our ability to think creatively, stay motivated, and expand our horizons. These strains offer a natural way to boost energy levels, improve mental clarity, and promote overall well-being, aligning us with Jupiter's expansive and optimistic qualities. Embracing the influence of Jupiter can lead to a life filled with growth, abundance, and endless possibilities.

Check out my Virtual dispensary for all your hemp needs: https://shift.store/sg1fan23477/retail

Chapter 7: Saturn: Discipline and Responsibility
Saturn's Role in Discipline and Responsibility

In astrology, Saturn is the planet that governs discipline, responsibility, and structure. Named after the Roman god of time and agriculture, Saturn represents the principles of limitation, order, and perseverance. It influences our sense of duty, our capacity for hard work, and our ability to endure challenges and restrictions.

Key Aspects of Saturn in Astrology:

1. **Discipline and Structure:** Saturn symbolizes the need for discipline, structure, and order in our lives. It teaches us the value of hard work, perseverance, and dedication.

2. **Responsibility and Duty:** Saturn governs our sense of responsibility and duty. It influences how we handle obligations, commitments, and the roles we play in society.

3. **Limitations and Challenges:** Saturn represents limitations, challenges, and obstacles. It teaches us to face difficulties with resilience and to learn from our experiences.

4. **Time and Patience:** Saturn is associated with time and the importance of patience. It emphasizes the need for long-term planning, delayed gratification, and the slow but steady progress toward our goals.

5. **Authority and Maturity:** Saturn embodies authority, maturity, and wisdom gained through experience. It influences our relationship with authority figures and our own capacity for leadership and self-mastery.

Saturn's Placement in the Zodiac:

- **Aries Saturn:** Disciplined, assertive, and pioneering. Aries Saturn individuals approach challenges with courage and determination, often taking the lead in difficult situations.
- **Taurus Saturn:** Persistent, practical, and reliable. Taurus Saturn individuals value stability and consistency, working diligently toward their goals.
- **Gemini Saturn:** Analytical, communicative, and adaptable. Gemini Saturn individuals approach responsibilities with intellectual curiosity and a focus on learning.
- **Cancer Saturn:** Protective, nurturing, and emotionally resilient. Cancer Saturn individuals are deeply committed to their family and home, often taking on significant responsibilities in these areas.
- **Leo Saturn:** Ambitious, disciplined, and authoritative. Leo Saturn individuals seek recognition and success through hard work and dedication, often taking on leadership roles.
- **Virgo Saturn:** Meticulous, organized, and service-oriented. Virgo Saturn individuals approach their duties with attention to detail and a strong desire to help others.
- **Libra Saturn:** Diplomatic, fair-minded, and cooperative. Libra Saturn individuals strive for balance and harmony in their responsibilities, often working to mediate conflicts and create fairness.
- **Scorpio Saturn:** Intense, focused, and transformative. Scorpio Saturn individuals face challenges with determination and a deep desire for personal growth and transformation.
- **Sagittarius Saturn:** Philosophical, disciplined, and optimistic. Sagittarius Saturn individuals approach their responsibilities with a sense of purpose and a desire to expand their horizons.
- **Capricorn Saturn:** Ambitious, disciplined, and pragmatic. Capricorn Saturn individuals are driven by a strong work ethic and a desire for achievement, often excelling in their careers.
- **Aquarius Saturn:** Innovative, independent, and progressive. Aquarius Saturn individuals approach their responsibilities with

a focus on innovation and social change, often challenging traditional structures.

- **Pisces Saturn:** Compassionate, intuitive, and creative. Pisces Saturn individuals approach their duties with empathy and a desire to help others, often finding unique and creative solutions to challenges.

Cannabis Strains for Focus and Grounding

Saturn's influence on discipline and responsibility makes it essential to find ways to enhance focus and grounding. Certain cannabis strains can help improve concentration, promote relaxation, and provide a sense of stability, aligning with the disciplined and structured nature of Saturn.

OG Kush: Relaxing and Grounding

OG Kush is a hybrid strain known for its potent relaxing effects and ability to provide a sense of grounding. It is ideal for those seeking to reduce stress and enhance focus.

- **Effects:** OG Kush offers a calming, euphoric high that helps to reduce stress and promote relaxation. Its grounding effects can enhance focus and provide a sense of stability, aligning well with Saturn's attributes of discipline and responsibility.
- **Flavor and Aroma:** This strain has a complex aroma with notes of earth, pine, and citrus, contributing to its soothing and grounding properties.
- **Usage:** OG Kush is suitable for evening use or during times of high stress, helping individuals to unwind and regain focus.

Bubba Kush: Calming and Focused

Bubba Kush is an indica strain known for its strong calming effects and ability to promote focus. It is perfect for those seeking deep relaxation and mental clarity.

- **Effects:** Bubba Kush provides a heavy, calming high that promotes deep relaxation and mental focus. Its sedative effects help to reduce anxiety and enhance concentration, making it a perfect complement to Saturn's disciplined and structured qualities.
- **Flavor and Aroma:** This strain has a sweet, earthy aroma with hints of coffee and chocolate, adding to its relaxing and grounding profile.
- **Usage:** Bubba Kush is best used in the evening or before bed to promote relaxation and focus, providing a sense of calm and clarity.

Northern Lights: Relaxing and Grounding

Northern Lights is a classic indica strain known for its deeply relaxing and calming effects. It is highly effective for those needing to unwind and achieve emotional tranquility.

- **Effects:** Northern Lights delivers a potent, body-focused high that promotes relaxation and sleep. Its calming effects help to alleviate stress, anxiety, and emotional tension, making it a perfect strain for grounding and focus.
- **Flavor and Aroma:** This strain has a sweet, earthy aroma with hints of pine and spice, adding to its comforting profile.
- **Usage:** Northern Lights is best used in the evening or before bed to help relax the body and mind, promoting restful sleep and emotional peace.

Granddaddy Purple: Relaxing and Clarifying

Granddaddy Purple is a popular indica strain known for its powerful relaxing effects and ability to alleviate stress and anxiety.

- **Effects:** Granddaddy Purple offers a calming, euphoric high that helps to reduce stress and promote relaxation. Its soothing effects make it an excellent choice for enhancing focus and grounding, aligning with Saturn's disciplined and responsible qualities.

- **Flavor and Aroma:** This strain has a sweet, grape-like aroma with earthy undertones, adding to its relaxing effects.
- **Usage:** Granddaddy Purple is best used in the evening to help unwind and relax after a stressful day, providing emotional comfort and peace.

Afghan Kush: Grounding and Soothing

Afghan Kush is a pure indica strain known for its potent calming effects and ability to promote a sense of grounding and relaxation.

- **Effects:** Afghan Kush provides a deep, soothing high that helps to reduce stress and promote mental clarity. Its grounding effects help to enhance focus and stability, making it a perfect complement to Saturn's disciplined and structured qualities.
- **Flavor and Aroma:** This strain has an earthy, woody aroma with hints of sweet and spicy notes, contributing to its calming and grounding profile.
- **Usage:** Afghan Kush is suitable for evening use or during times of high stress, helping individuals to unwind and regain focus.

Conclusion

Saturn in astrology governs our sense of discipline, responsibility, and structure. Understanding its influence can help us enhance our ability to focus, maintain grounding, and approach our duties with dedication and perseverance. By integrating specific cannabis strains that promote relaxation, focus, and grounding, such as OG Kush, Bubba Kush, Northern Lights, Granddaddy Purple, and Afghan Kush, we can align ourselves with Saturn's disciplined and responsible qualities. These strains offer a natural way to reduce stress, improve concentration, and promote overall well-being, empowering us to tackle our responsibilities with clarity and resilience. Embracing the influence of Saturn can lead to a life filled with order, achievement, and personal growth.

Check out my Virtual dispensary for all your hemp needs: https://shift.store/sg1fan23477/retail

Chapter 8: Uranus: Innovation and Change

Uranus's Influence on Innovation and Change

In astrology, Uranus is the planet that governs innovation, change, and the unconventional. Named after the ancient Greek god of the sky, Uranus represents the principles of rebellion, originality, and sudden shifts. It influences our desire to break free from tradition, embrace new ideas, and seek out unique experiences.

Key Aspects of Uranus in Astrology:

1. **Innovation and Originality:** Uranus symbolizes the drive for innovation and originality. It encourages us to think outside the box, explore new concepts, and embrace cutting-edge ideas.
2. **Change and Rebellion:** Uranus governs change and rebellion against the status quo. It inspires us to challenge existing structures and seek out transformative experiences.
3. **Freedom and Independence:** Uranus represents the desire for freedom and independence. It influences our need to break free from limitations and pursue our own path.
4. **Sudden Events and Surprises:** Uranus is associated with sudden events and unexpected changes. It brings about shifts that can disrupt our routine and force us to adapt quickly.
5. **Humanitarianism and Social Progress:** Uranus embodies humanitarian ideals and the pursuit of social progress. It drives us to advocate for equality, justice, and positive change in society.

Uranus's Placement in the Zodiac:

- **Aries Uranus:** Bold, pioneering, and assertive. Aries Uranus individuals seek innovation through action and are often at the forefront of change.

- **Taurus Uranus:** Practical, grounded, and resourceful. Taurus Uranus individuals approach innovation with practicality, focusing on sustainable and tangible results.
- **Gemini Uranus:** Curious, communicative, and adaptable. Gemini Uranus individuals are mentally agile and thrive on new ideas and intellectual exploration.
- **Cancer Uranus:** Intuitive, nurturing, and emotionally insightful. Cancer Uranus individuals seek change that enhances emotional well-being and family dynamics.
- **Leo Uranus:** Dramatic, creative, and charismatic. Leo Uranus individuals innovate through self-expression and creative endeavors, often inspiring others.
- **Virgo Uranus:** Analytical, detail-oriented, and service-minded. Virgo Uranus individuals approach innovation through meticulous planning and a desire to improve systems.
- **Libra Uranus:** Diplomatic, balanced, and fair-minded. Libra Uranus individuals seek innovation that promotes harmony and equality in relationships and society.
- **Scorpio Uranus:** Intense, transformative, and secretive. Scorpio Uranus individuals drive deep, transformative change, often through exploring hidden truths.
- **Sagittarius Uranus:** Adventurous, optimistic, and philosophical. Sagittarius Uranus individuals pursue innovation through exploration and expanding their horizons.
- **Capricorn Uranus:** Ambitious, disciplined, and strategic. Capricorn Uranus individuals approach innovation with a focus on long-term goals and practical implementation.
- **Aquarius Uranus:** Innovative, independent, and humanitarian. Aquarius Uranus individuals are visionaries who seek to revolutionize society and advocate for social progress.
- **Pisces Uranus:** Compassionate, imaginative, and intuitive. Pisces Uranus individuals pursue innovation through creative and spiritual avenues, often blending reality with fantasy.

Cannabis Strains for Creativity and Innovation

Uranus's influence on innovation and change makes it essential to find ways to enhance creativity and embrace new ideas. Certain cannabis strains can boost creativity, inspire new concepts, and promote a sense of well-being, aligning with the innovative and unconventional nature of Uranus.

Pineapple Express: Energizing and Creative

Pineapple Express is a hybrid strain known for its balanced effects, offering both mental stimulation and physical relaxation. It is a favorite for those seeking a harmonious blend of energy and creativity.

- **Effects:** Pineapple Express provides a mild, euphoric high that promotes happiness and creativity. It enhances focus and productivity while also offering a subtle body relaxation, making it a versatile strain that resonates with Uranus's attributes of innovation and change.
- **Flavor and Aroma:** This strain has a delightful tropical aroma with hints of pineapple and citrus, contributing to its refreshing and enjoyable effects.
- **Usage:** Pineapple Express is suitable for any time of day, particularly when a balanced approach to energy and relaxation is desired, helping to spark creativity and innovative thinking.

Sour Tangie: Uplifting and Energizing

Sour Tangie is a sativa-dominant hybrid known for its potent, uplifting effects and tangy citrus flavor. It is perfect for those seeking an energy boost and enhanced mood.

- **Effects:** Sour Tangie delivers a strong, cerebral high that enhances focus, creativity, and motivation. Its energizing effects help combat fatigue and promote a sense of enthusiasm and optimism, aligning with Uranus's growth-oriented nature.

- **Flavor and Aroma:** This strain has a tangy, citrusy aroma with sweet undertones, adding to its invigorating profile.
- **Usage:** Sour Tangie is ideal for daytime use, providing a sustained boost in energy and mental sharpness, helping individuals stay active and engaged.

Super Silver Haze: Creative and Energizing

Super Silver Haze is a sativa-dominant hybrid known for its up-lifting and mood-enhancing effects. It is perfect for those needing an emotional boost and mental clarity.

- **Effects:** Super Silver Haze delivers a cerebral, euphoric high that enhances mood and energy levels. It helps to reduce stress and anxiety while promoting a positive, optimistic outlook, aligning with Uranus's innovative and forward-thinking qualities.
- **Flavor and Aroma:** This strain has a spicy, citrusy aroma with earthy undertones, contributing to its invigorating effects.
- **Usage:** Super Silver Haze is suitable for daytime use, providing a boost in energy and mood without causing sedation, helping to spark creativity and innovative thinking.

Green Crack: Energizing and Motivating

Green Crack, despite its controversial name, is a pure sativa strain famed for its sharp, invigorating effects. It is ideal for those needing a substantial energy boost and mental clarity.

- **Effects:** Green Crack delivers a potent cerebral high that enhances focus, energy, and motivation. Its effects are long-lasting and can help combat stress and fatigue, making it an excellent comple-ment to Uranus's drive for innovation and change.
- **Flavor and Aroma:** This strain has a tangy, fruity flavor reminis-cent of mango, with an earthy undertone that adds to its vibrant profile.

- **Usage:** Green Crack is best used during the day when mental alertness and physical activity are required, helping individuals tackle tasks with enthusiasm and vigor.

Jack Herer: Creative and Euphoric

Named after the famous cannabis activist, Jack Herer is a well-balanced hybrid strain known for its potent, clear-headed effects and ability to enhance creativity and concentration.

- **Effects:** Jack Herer offers a blissful, euphoric high that stimulates both the mind and body. It promotes a sense of well-being and encourages creative thinking, making it a perfect complement to Uranus's role in driving innovation and change.
- **Flavor and Aroma:** The strain has a distinctive aroma with notes of pine, earth, and citrus, contributing to its refreshing and energizing effects.
- **Usage:** Jack Herer is often used during creative endeavors or social activities, providing a burst of energy and inspiration without overwhelming the senses.

Conclusion

Uranus in astrology governs our drive for innovation, change, and the unconventional. Understanding its influence can help us embrace new ideas, think outside the box, and pursue unique experiences with confidence. By integrating specific cannabis strains that promote creativity, energy, and mental clarity, such as Pineapple Express, Sour Tangie, Super Silver Haze, Green Crack, and Jack Herer, we can align ourselves with Uranus's innovative and transformative qualities. These strains offer a natural way to boost creativity, reduce stress, and promote overall well-being, empowering us to tackle challenges, explore new concepts, and live with originality and enthusiasm. Embracing the influence of Uranus can lead to a life filled with innovation, progress, and unexpected opportunities.

Check out my Virtual dispensary for all your hemp needs: https://shift.store/sg1fan23477/retail

Chapter 9: Neptune: Dreams and Spirituality
Neptune's Impact on Dreams and Spirituality

In astrology, Neptune is the planet that governs dreams, spirituality, and the subconscious. Named after the Roman god of the sea, Neptune represents the principles of illusion, intuition, and mysticism. It influences our connection to the spiritual realm, our imagination, and our ability to perceive beyond the physical world.

Key Aspects of Neptune in Astrology:

1. **Dreams and Imagination:** Neptune symbolizes the realm of dreams and imagination. It encourages us to explore our inner worlds, creative potential, and the power of our subconscious mind.

2. **Spirituality and Mysticism:** Neptune governs spirituality and mysticism, influencing our connection to the divine, our spiritual beliefs, and our quest for higher understanding.

3. **Intuition and Psychic Abilities:** Neptune enhances our intuition and psychic abilities. It helps us tune into subtle energies and gain insights that transcend logical reasoning.

4. **Illusion and Delusion:** Neptune also represents illusion and delusion, teaching us to discern reality from fantasy and navigate the blurry line between truth and deception.

5. **Compassion and Empathy:** Neptune embodies compassion and empathy, driving us to connect with others on a deep, emotional level and to express unconditional love.

Neptune's Placement in the Zodiac:

- **Aries Neptune:** Idealistic, visionary, and pioneering. Aries Neptune individuals are driven by bold spiritual visions and a desire to break new ground in their quest for understanding.
- **Taurus Neptune:** Practical, sensual, and grounded. Taurus Neptune individuals seek spiritual experiences through nature, beauty, and the physical senses.
- **Gemini Neptune:** Curious, communicative, and versatile. Gemini Neptune individuals explore spirituality through intellectual pursuits, communication, and the exchange of ideas.
- **Cancer Neptune:** Intuitive, nurturing, and emotionally insightful. Cancer Neptune individuals connect with spirituality through their emotions, family, and home.
- **Leo Neptune:** Dramatic, creative, and charismatic. Leo Neptune individuals express their spirituality through creative endeavors and a desire to inspire others.
- **Virgo Neptune:** Analytical, detail-oriented, and service-minded. Virgo Neptune individuals approach spirituality with a focus on healing, service, and practical applications.
- **Libra Neptune:** Diplomatic, balanced, and fair-minded. Libra Neptune individuals seek spiritual harmony and balance in their relationships and social interactions.
- **Scorpio Neptune:** Intense, transformative, and secretive. Scorpio Neptune individuals explore spirituality through deep, transformative experiences and a desire to uncover hidden truths.
- **Sagittarius Neptune:** Adventurous, optimistic, and philosophical. Sagittarius Neptune individuals pursue spiritual growth through exploration, travel, and expanding their horizons.
- **Capricorn Neptune:** Ambitious, disciplined, and pragmatic. Capricorn Neptune individuals seek to integrate spirituality into their practical goals and long-term plans.
- **Aquarius Neptune:** Innovative, independent, and humanitarian. Aquarius Neptune individuals are visionaries who seek to revolutionize spirituality and advocate for social progress.

- **Pisces Neptune:** Compassionate, empathetic, and dreamy. Pisces Neptune individuals are deeply connected to their intuition and spiritual realms, often blending reality with fantasy.

Cannabis Strains for Enhancing Spiritual Experiences

Neptune's influence on dreams and spirituality makes it essential to find ways to deepen our spiritual connections and enhance our intuitive abilities. Certain cannabis strains can promote relaxation, enhance spiritual experiences, and facilitate a sense of inner peace, aligning with the mystical and compassionate nature of Neptune.

Lavender: Tranquil and Spiritual

Lavender is an indica-dominant strain known for its strong calming and sedative effects. It is ideal for those seeking deep relaxation and enhanced spiritual experiences.

- **Effects:** Lavender provides a heavy, tranquilizing high that eases the mind and body into a state of deep relaxation. Its calming effects help to quiet the mind and promote a sense of peace, making it perfect for meditation and spiritual practices.
- **Flavor and Aroma:** This strain has a floral, lavender-like aroma with hints of herbs and spices, enhancing its soothing properties.
- **Usage:** Lavender is best used in the evening or during spiritual practices to promote relaxation, inner peace, and a deep connection to the spiritual realm.

Purple Kush: Relaxing and Meditative

Purple Kush is an indica strain known for its deeply relaxing and calming effects. It is highly effective for those seeking to unwind and achieve a meditative state.

- **Effects:** Purple Kush delivers a potent, body-focused high that promotes relaxation and tranquility. Its calming effects help to reduce stress and enhance introspection, making it a perfect strain for meditation and spiritual exploration.

- **Flavor and Aroma:** This strain has a sweet, earthy aroma with hints of grape and berry, contributing to its comforting profile.
- **Usage:** Purple Kush is best used in the evening or during meditation to help relax the body and mind, promoting a meditative and spiritual experience.

Blueberry: Euphoric and Relaxing

Blueberry is an indica-dominant strain known for its relaxing and euphoric effects. It is perfect for those seeking a sense of well-being and spiritual connection.

- **Effects:** Blueberry offers a calming, euphoric high that promotes relaxation and happiness. Its soothing effects can enhance feelings of love and connection, making it ideal for spiritual practices and meditation.
- **Flavor and Aroma:** This strain has a sweet, berry-like aroma with earthy undertones, adding to its delightful sensory experience.
- **Usage:** Blueberry is suitable for any time of day, providing relaxation and a positive mood that enhances spiritual and meditative practices.

White Widow: Balanced and Introspective

White Widow is a balanced hybrid strain known for its uplifting and calming effects. It is ideal for those seeking to enhance their spiritual and introspective experiences.

- **Effects:** White Widow provides a balanced high that promotes mental clarity and relaxation. Its uplifting effects help to reduce stress and enhance introspection, making it perfect for meditation and spiritual practices.

- **Flavor and Aroma:** This strain has a pungent, earthy aroma with hints of pine and spice, contributing to its calming and grounding profile.
- **Usage:** White Widow is suitable for any time of day, providing a balanced approach to relaxation and mental clarity, helping to deepen spiritual and meditative experiences.

Amnesia Haze: Uplifting and Spiritual

Amnesia Haze is a sativa-dominant strain known for its uplifting and mood-enhancing effects. It is perfect for those seeking an emotional boost and enhanced spiritual connection.

- **Effects:** Amnesia Haze delivers a cerebral, euphoric high that enhances mood and energy levels. It helps to reduce stress and anxiety while promoting a positive, optimistic outlook, aligning with Neptune's spiritual and intuitive qualities.
- **Flavor and Aroma:** This strain has a citrusy, earthy aroma with hints of sweetness, contributing to its uplifting effects.
- **Usage:** Amnesia Haze is suitable for daytime use, providing a boost in energy and mood without causing sedation, helping to spark creativity and spiritual insights.

Conclusion

Neptune in astrology governs our dreams, spirituality, and connection to the subconscious. Understanding its influence can help us deepen our spiritual practices, enhance our intuitive abilities, and navigate the realm of dreams and imagination with greater awareness. By integrating specific cannabis strains that promote relaxation, spiritual connection, and mental clarity, such as Lavender, Purple Kush, Blueberry, White Widow, and Amnesia Haze, we can align ourselves with Neptune's mystical and compassionate qualities. These strains offer a natural way to reduce stress, enhance introspection, and promote overall well-being, empowering us to explore our inner worlds, connect with the divine, and embrace our spiritual journey with openness and curiosity. Embracing the influence of Neptune can lead to a life filled with dreams, spiritual insights, and a profound connection to the universe.

Check out my Virtual dispensary for all your hemp needs: https://shift.store/sg1fan23477/retail

Chapter 10: Pluto: Transformation and Power
Pluto's Role in Transformation and Power

In astrology, Pluto is the planet that governs transformation, power, and rebirth. Named after the Roman god of the underworld, Pluto represents the principles of deep change, regeneration, and the cyclical nature of life. It influences our ability to undergo profound transformations, confront our inner shadows, and emerge stronger and more powerful.

Key Aspects of Pluto in Astrology:

1. **Transformation and Rebirth:** Pluto symbolizes profound transformation and rebirth. It encourages us to undergo deep, often challenging changes that lead to personal growth and renewal.
2. **Power and Control:** Pluto governs power dynamics, control, and the use of influence. It highlights our relationship with power, both personal and external, and how we wield it.
3. **Intensity and Depth:** Pluto represents intensity and depth, influencing our capacity for deep emotional experiences and the exploration of hidden truths.
4. **Shadow and Unconscious:** Pluto is associated with the shadow self and the unconscious mind. It drives us to confront and integrate our hidden fears, desires, and traumas.
5. **Regeneration and Healing:** Pluto embodies the principles of regeneration and healing. It influences our ability to recover from difficulties, heal from past wounds, and emerge stronger.

Pluto's Placement in the Zodiac:

- **Aries Pluto:** Bold, pioneering, and assertive. Aries Pluto individuals undergo transformation through bold actions and pioneering endeavors.
- **Taurus Pluto:** Persistent, resourceful, and grounded. Taurus Pluto individuals experience transformation through material stability and resourcefulness.
- **Gemini Pluto:** Curious, communicative, and adaptable. Gemini Pluto individuals seek transformation through intellectual exploration and communication.
- **Cancer Pluto:** Intuitive, nurturing, and emotionally insightful. Cancer Pluto individuals undergo transformation through deep emotional connections and family dynamics.
- **Leo Pluto:** Dramatic, creative, and charismatic. Leo Pluto individuals experience transformation through self-expression and creative endeavors.
- **Virgo Pluto:** Analytical, detail-oriented, and service-minded. Virgo Pluto individuals seek transformation through healing, service, and practical improvements.
- **Libra Pluto:** Diplomatic, balanced, and fair-minded. Libra Pluto individuals undergo transformation through relationships and the pursuit of harmony and balance.
- **Scorpio Pluto:** Intense, transformative, and secretive. Scorpio Pluto individuals experience profound transformation through deep emotional and psychological exploration.
- **Sagittarius Pluto:** Adventurous, optimistic, and philosophical. Sagittarius Pluto individuals seek transformation through exploration, travel, and expanding their horizons.
- **Capricorn Pluto:** Ambitious, disciplined, and pragmatic. Capricorn Pluto individuals undergo transformation through hard work, discipline, and achieving long-term goals.
- **Aquarius Pluto:** Innovative, independent, and humanitarian. Aquarius Pluto individuals seek transformation through revolutionary ideas and social progress.

- **Pisces Pluto:** Compassionate, empathetic, and dreamy. Pisces Pluto individuals experience transformation through spiritual and creative pursuits.

Cannabis Strains for Deep Transformation

Pluto's influence on transformation and power makes it essential to find ways to facilitate deep personal growth and healing. Certain cannabis strains can promote introspection, emotional release, and profound transformation, aligning with the intense and regenerative nature of Pluto.

Gorilla Glue: Intense and Transformative

Gorilla Glue, also known as GG4, is a potent hybrid strain known for its powerful effects and ability to promote deep relaxation and introspection. It is ideal for those seeking profound transformation and emotional release.

- **Effects:** Gorilla Glue delivers a heavy, euphoric high that promotes deep relaxation and mental clarity. Its intense effects help to alleviate stress and anxiety, making it perfect for deep introspection and personal transformation.
- **Flavor and Aroma:** This strain has a pungent, earthy aroma with hints of pine and sour notes, contributing to its grounding and transformative properties.
- **Usage:** Gorilla Glue is best used in the evening or during periods of high stress, helping individuals to unwind and engage in deep introspection and emotional release.

Trainwreck: Energizing and Mind-Expanding

Trainwreck is a sativa-dominant hybrid strain known for its potent, mind-expanding effects and ability to promote creativity and introspection. It is perfect for those seeking profound transformation and mental clarity.

- **Effects:** Trainwreck provides a strong, cerebral high that enhances focus, creativity, and motivation. Its intense effects help to reduce stress and promote a sense of mental clarity, making it ideal for deep personal transformation and emotional healing.
- **Flavor and Aroma:** This strain has a pungent, earthy aroma with hints of pine and citrus, contributing to its invigorating and transformative profile.
- **Usage:** Trainwreck is suitable for daytime use, providing a sustained boost in energy and mental sharpness, helping individuals engage in introspection and personal growth.

Blue Dream: Relaxing and Uplifting

Blue Dream is a hybrid strain celebrated for its balanced effects that provide both relaxation and mental invigoration. It is an excellent choice for those seeking to enhance creativity and stress relief during transformational periods.

- **Effects:** Blue Dream offers a gentle, euphoric high that helps to calm the mind and uplift the spirit. It provides a sense of mental clarity and relaxation without sedation, making it ideal for creative projects and personal growth.
- **Flavor and Aroma:** This strain has a sweet, berry-like aroma with earthy undertones, contributing to its soothing effects.
- **Usage:** Blue Dream is suitable for any time of day, providing emotional stability and a positive mindset without overwhelming the senses, supporting deep transformation and healing.

Purple Kush: Calming and Meditative

Purple Kush is an indica strain known for its deeply relaxing and calming effects. It is highly effective for those seeking to unwind and achieve a meditative state during transformational periods.

- **Effects:** Purple Kush delivers a potent, body-focused high that promotes relaxation and tranquility. Its calming effects help to reduce stress and enhance introspection, making it a perfect strain for meditation and spiritual exploration.
- **Flavor and Aroma:** This strain has a sweet, earthy aroma with hints of grape and berry, contributing to its comforting profile.
- **Usage:** Purple Kush is best used in the evening or during meditation to help relax the body and mind, promoting a meditative and transformative experience.

Northern Lights: Relaxing and Grounding

Northern Lights is a classic indica strain known for its deeply relaxing and calming effects. It is highly effective for those needing to unwind and achieve emotional tranquility during periods of transformation.

- **Effects:** Northern Lights delivers a potent, body-focused high that promotes relaxation and sleep. Its calming effects help to alleviate stress, anxiety, and emotional tension, making it a perfect strain for grounding and deep transformation.
- **Flavor and Aroma:** This strain has a sweet, earthy aroma with hints of pine and spice, adding to its comforting profile.
- **Usage:** Northern Lights is best used in the evening or before bed to help relax the body and mind, promoting restful sleep and emotional peace during transformational periods.

Conclusion

Pluto in astrology governs our capacity for deep transformation, power, and regeneration. Understanding its influence can help us embrace profound changes, confront our inner shadows, and emerge stronger and more empowered. By integrating specific cannabis strains that promote relaxation, introspection, and mental clarity, such as Gorilla Glue, Trainwreck, Blue Dream, Purple Kush, and Northern Lights, we can align ourselves with Pluto's transformative and regenerative qualities. These strains offer a natural way to reduce stress, enhance introspection, and promote overall well-being, empowering us to tackle challenges, explore new concepts, and live with originality and enthusiasm. Embracing the influence of Pluto can lead to a life filled with profound transformation, personal growth, and a deeper connection to our inner power.

Check out my Virtual dispensary for all your hemp needs: https://shift.store/sg1fan23477/retail

Part II: The Zodiac Signs and Their Traits

Chapter 11: Aries: The Pioneer

Traits of Aries

Aries, the first sign of the zodiac, is known as the pioneer. Governed by Mars, the planet of action and energy, Aries embodies the spirit of initiation, courage, and enthusiasm. As a cardinal fire sign, Aries is dynamic, bold, and always ready to blaze new trails. Understanding the core traits of Aries can help us appreciate the vibrant energy and leadership qualities that define this sign.

Key Traits of Aries:

1. **Leadership and Initiative:** Aries individuals are natural leaders. They are not afraid to take charge and are often the first to start new projects and ventures. Their pioneering spirit drives them to explore uncharted territories and set new trends.

2. **Courage and Determination:** Courage is a hallmark of Aries. They face challenges head-on and are not easily deterred by obstacles. Their determination ensures they persist until their goals are achieved.

3. **Enthusiasm and Energy:** Aries possesses boundless energy and enthusiasm. They approach life with excitement and are always eager to take on new adventures. Their zest for life is infectious and inspiring.

4. **Independence and Self-Reliance:** Aries values independence and self-reliance. They prefer to forge their own path and make their own decisions. Their strong sense of self ensures they are confident and assertive in their actions.

5. **Impulsiveness and Impatience:** While their impulsiveness can lead to spontaneous and exciting actions, it can also result in hasty decisions. Aries individuals may struggle with patience and often seek immediate results.

6. **Honesty and Directness:** Aries is known for their honesty and directness. They speak their mind openly and are not afraid to express their opinions. This straightforward approach can sometimes come across as blunt, but it is rooted in their desire for authenticity.

7. **Competitive Nature:** Aries is highly competitive and thrives in situations that require them to prove their skills and abilities. They enjoy challenges and are driven by a desire to be the best.

Aries in Relationships:

- **Romantic Relationships:** In romantic relationships, Aries is passionate, adventurous, and affectionate. They seek excitement and are always looking for ways to keep the romance alive. Their partners can expect spontaneous gestures of love and a dynamic, energetic connection.

- **Friendships:** As friends, Aries is loyal, supportive, and fun-loving. They are the life of the party and enjoy engaging in exciting activities with their friends. They are always ready to lend a helping hand and offer honest advice.

- **Family:** Within the family, Aries takes on a protective and nurturing role. They are fiercely loyal to their loved ones and are always ready to stand up for them. Their energy and enthusiasm often inspire and uplift their family members.

- **Career:** In their careers, Aries excels in roles that require leadership, creativity, and initiative. They are not afraid to take risks and are often found in pioneering positions where they can innovate and drive progress.

Best Cannabis Strains for Aries

Given the dynamic and energetic nature of Aries, the best cannabis strains for this sign should enhance their natural qualities and provide balance where needed. Strains that promote focus, creativity, and relaxation can help Aries harness their energy and maintain their drive without burning out.

Jack Herer: Energizing and Creative

Named after the famous cannabis activist, Jack Herer is a sativa-dominant strain renowned for its clear-headed and creative effects. It is an excellent choice for Aries individuals who seek to enhance their energy and creativity.

- **Effects:** Jack Herer offers a blissful, euphoric high that stimulates both the mind and body. It promotes a sense of well-being and encourages creative thinking, making it perfect for Aries's dynamic and innovative nature.
- **Flavor and Aroma:** The strain has a distinctive aroma with notes of pine, earth, and citrus, contributing to its refreshing and energizing effects.
- **Usage:** Jack Herer is suitable for daytime use, providing a burst of energy and inspiration without overwhelming the senses. It helps Aries stay focused and driven throughout the day.

Girl Scout Cookies: Balanced and Euphoric

Girl Scout Cookies (GSC) is a hybrid strain known for its balanced effects that provide both relaxation and mental invigoration. It is an excellent choice for Aries individuals who seek to enhance their focus and relaxation while maintaining their dynamic energy.

- **Effects:** Girl Scout Cookies offers a euphoric high that promotes happiness and relaxation. Its balanced effects help to reduce stress and anxiety, making it ideal for Aries's high-energy lifestyle.

- **Flavor and Aroma:** This strain has a sweet, earthy aroma with hints of mint and spices, contributing to its soothing and enjoyable experience.
- **Usage:** Girl Scout Cookies is suitable for any time of day, providing relaxation and a positive mood that helps Aries unwind and recharge without losing their edge.

Durban Poison: Pure Energy and Focus

Durban Poison is a pure sativa strain originating from South Africa, known for its invigorating and uplifting effects. It is perfect for Aries individuals seeking a natural boost in energy and mental clarity.

- **Effects:** Durban Poison delivers a strong, cerebral high that enhances focus, creativity, and productivity. Its energizing effects help combat fatigue and promote a sense of motivation and enthusiasm, aligning perfectly with Aries's dynamic and assertive nature.
- **Flavor and Aroma:** This strain has a sweet, earthy aroma with hints of pine and spice, adding to its invigorating profile.
- **Usage:** Durban Poison is ideal for daytime use, providing a sustained boost in energy and mental sharpness, helping Aries stay active and engaged.

Sour Diesel: Uplifting and Euphoric

Sour Diesel is a sativa-dominant strain renowned for its fast-acting, energizing effects. It is a popular choice for Aries individuals who seek to enhance vitality and mental clarity.

- **Effects:** Sour Diesel provides an uplifting and euphoric high, making it ideal for combating fatigue and promoting a positive mindset. It can help spark creativity and motivation, aligning well with Aries's need for action and excitement.

- **Flavor and Aroma:** This strain has a pungent diesel-like aroma with hints of citrus and earthiness, adding to its invigorating profile.
- **Usage:** Sour Diesel is suitable for daytime use, helping Aries stay active, focused, and inspired throughout the day.

Pineapple Express: Balanced and Euphoric

Pineapple Express is a hybrid strain known for its balanced effects, offering both mental stimulation and physical relaxation. It is a favorite for Aries individuals who seek a harmonious blend of energy and calmness.

- **Effects:** Pineapple Express provides a mild, euphoric high that promotes happiness and creativity. It enhances focus and productivity while also offering a subtle body relaxation, making it a versatile strain that resonates with Aries's vibrant and dynamic nature.
- **Flavor and Aroma:** This strain has a delightful tropical aroma with hints of pineapple and citrus, contributing to its refreshing and enjoyable effects.
- **Usage:** Pineapple Express is suitable for any time of day, particularly when a balanced approach to energy and relaxation is desired, helping Aries stay motivated and grounded.

Conclusion

Aries, the pioneer of the zodiac, is defined by their dynamic energy, leadership qualities, and adventurous spirit. Understanding their core traits can help us appreciate their vibrant and assertive nature. By integrating specific cannabis strains that promote energy, creativity, and relaxation, such as Jack Herer, Girl Scout Cookies, Durban Poison, Sour Diesel, and Pineapple Express, Aries individuals can enhance their natural qualities and maintain their drive without burning out. These strains offer a natural way to boost focus, reduce stress, and promote overall well-being, empowering Aries to lead, innovate, and explore with confidence and enthusiasm. Embracing the influence of Aries can lead to a life filled with excitement, growth, and endless possibilities.

Check out my Virtual dispensary for all your hemp needs: https://shift.store/sg1fan23477/retail

Chapter 12: Taurus: The Builder
Traits of Taurus

Taurus, the second sign of the zodiac, is known as the builder. Governed by Venus, the planet of love, beauty, and abundance, Taurus embodies the principles of stability, sensuality, and practicality. As a fixed earth sign, Taurus is grounded, patient, and determined, with a strong appreciation for the finer things in life. Understanding the core traits of Taurus can help us appreciate their reliable and steadfast nature.

Key Traits of Taurus:

1. **Stability and Reliability:** Taurus individuals are known for their stability and reliability. They are the rock upon which others can depend, always consistent and dependable in their actions and decisions.

2. **Patience and Perseverance:** Patience is a hallmark of Taurus. They understand that good things take time and are willing to wait and work diligently towards their goals. Their perseverance ensures they achieve what they set out to do.

3. **Sensuality and Appreciation for Beauty:** Ruled by Venus, Taurus has a heightened appreciation for beauty and sensual pleasures. They enjoy indulging in good food, art, music, and all forms of aesthetic pleasure.

4. **Practicality and Resourcefulness:** Taurus is highly practical and resourceful. They approach life with a pragmatic mindset, focusing on what is tangible and achievable.

5. **Determination and Tenacity:** Taurus possesses a strong will and determination. Once they set their mind on something, they are tenacious in their pursuit, often achieving their goals through sheer persistence.

6. **Love of Comfort and Security:** Taurus values comfort and security, both materially and emotionally. They seek to create

a stable and comfortable environment for themselves and their loved ones.

7. **Loyalty and Trustworthiness:** Taurus is fiercely loyal and trustworthy. They build strong, lasting relationships and are always there for their friends and family in times of need.

Taurus in Relationships:

- **Romantic Relationships:** In romantic relationships, Taurus is affectionate, loyal, and attentive. They seek stability and long-term commitment, often providing a solid and nurturing foundation for their partners. Their love for sensual pleasures makes them romantic and indulgent partners.
- **Friendships:** As friends, Taurus is dependable, supportive, and caring. They enjoy spending quality time with friends, often organizing gatherings and events to bring people together. Their loyalty ensures they are always there for their friends.
- **Family:** Within the family, Taurus takes on a protective and nurturing role. They value family traditions and work hard to provide comfort and security for their loved ones. Their patience and reliability make them strong pillars in the family unit.
- **Career:** In their careers, Taurus excels in roles that require persistence, practicality, and attention to detail. They are often found in professions related to finance, real estate, art, and agriculture, where they can apply their resourcefulness and appreciation for beauty.

Best Cannabis Strains for Taurus

Given the grounded and sensual nature of Taurus, the best cannabis strains for this sign should enhance their natural qualities and provide relaxation and comfort. Strains that promote relaxation, stress relief, and an appreciation for sensory experiences can help Taurus unwind and enjoy their surroundings.

Granddaddy Purple: Relaxing and Comforting

Granddaddy Purple (GDP) is an indica strain known for its deeply relaxing and soothing effects. It is an excellent choice for Taurus individuals who seek comfort and stress relief.

- **Effects:** Granddaddy Purple offers a calming, euphoric high that promotes relaxation and sleep. Its powerful effects help to reduce stress and anxiety, making it perfect for Taurus's love of comfort and relaxation.
- **Flavor and Aroma:** This strain has a sweet, grape-like aroma with earthy undertones, contributing to its comforting and enjoyable experience.
- **Usage:** Granddaddy Purple is best used in the evening or before bed to help Taurus unwind and achieve a deep, restful sleep.

Northern Lights: Calming and Grounding

Northern Lights is a classic indica strain known for its deeply relaxing and calming effects. It is highly effective for those needing to unwind and achieve emotional tranquility.

- **Effects:** Northern Lights delivers a potent, body-focused high that promotes relaxation and sleep. Its calming effects help to alleviate stress, anxiety, and emotional tension, making it a perfect strain for grounding and focus.
- **Flavor and Aroma:** This strain has a sweet, earthy aroma with hints of pine and spice, adding to its comforting profile.
- **Usage:** Northern Lights is best used in the evening or before bed to help relax the body and mind, promoting restful sleep and emotional peace.

Blueberry: Euphoric and Relaxing

Blueberry is an indica-dominant strain known for its relaxing and euphoric effects. It is perfect for those seeking a sense of well-being and sensory enjoyment.

- **Effects:** Blueberry offers a calming, euphoric high that promotes relaxation and happiness. Its soothing effects can enhance feelings of contentment and sensory appreciation, making it ideal for Taurus's love of beauty and comfort.
- **Flavor and Aroma:** This strain has a sweet, berry-like aroma with earthy undertones, adding to its delightful sensory experience.
- **Usage:** Blueberry is suitable for any time of day, providing relaxation and a positive mood that enhances Taurus's enjoyment of their surroundings.

Bubba Kush: Calming and Grounded

Bubba Kush is an indica strain known for its strong calming effects and ability to promote relaxation. It is perfect for those seeking deep relaxation and mental clarity.

- **Effects:** Bubba Kush provides a heavy, calming high that promotes deep relaxation and stress relief. Its sedative effects help to reduce anxiety and enhance concentration, making it a perfect complement to Taurus's need for comfort and stability.
- **Flavor and Aroma:** This strain has a sweet, earthy aroma with hints of coffee and chocolate, adding to its relaxing and grounding profile.
- **Usage:** Bubba Kush is best used in the evening or before bed to promote relaxation and focus, providing a sense of calm and clarity.

Purple Kush: Deeply Relaxing and Soothing

Purple Kush is an indica strain known for its deeply relaxing and calming effects. It is highly effective for those seeking to unwind and achieve a meditative state during transformational periods.

- **Effects:** Purple Kush delivers a potent, body-focused high that promotes relaxation and tranquility. Its calming effects help to reduce stress and enhance introspection, making it a perfect strain for meditation and spiritual exploration.
- **Flavor and Aroma:** This strain has a sweet, earthy aroma with hints of grape and berry, contributing to its comforting profile.
- **Usage:** Purple Kush is best used in the evening or during meditation to help relax the body and mind, promoting a meditative and transformative experience.

Conclusion

Taurus, the builder of the zodiac, is defined by their stability, patience, and appreciation for beauty and comfort. Understanding their core traits can help us appreciate their reliable and steadfast nature. By integrating specific cannabis strains that promote relaxation, stress relief, and sensory enjoyment, such as Granddaddy Purple, Northern Lights, Blueberry, Bubba Kush, and Purple Kush, Taurus individuals can enhance their natural qualities and find comfort and relaxation in their daily lives. These strains offer a natural way to boost relaxation, reduce stress, and promote overall well-being, empowering Taurus to build a life filled with beauty, comfort, and lasting satisfaction. Embracing the influence of Taurus can lead to a life filled with stability, growth, and an appreciation for the finer things in life.

Check out my Virtual dispensary for all your hemp needs: https://shift.store/sg1fan23477/retail

Chapter 13: Gemini: The Communicator
Traits of Gemini

Gemini, the third sign of the zodiac, is known as the communicator. Governed by Mercury, the planet of communication, intellect, and agility, Gemini embodies the principles of curiosity, adaptability, and sociability. As a mutable air sign, Gemini is dynamic, versatile, and always eager to learn and share information. Understanding the core traits of Gemini can help us appreciate their vibrant and intellectually stimulating nature.

Key Traits of Gemini:

1. **Curiosity and Intellect:** Gemini individuals are naturally curious and intellectually driven. They have an insatiable thirst for knowledge and enjoy learning about a wide range of topics.
2. **Adaptability and Versatility:** Adaptability is a hallmark of Gemini. They can easily adjust to new situations and are comfortable with change. Their versatility allows them to thrive in various environments and roles.
3. **Communication and Sociability:** Gemini excels in communication and sociability. They are articulate, expressive, and enjoy engaging in conversations. Their ability to connect with others makes them excellent communicators and networkers.
4. **Wit and Humor:** Gemini possesses a sharp wit and a great sense of humor. They enjoy making others laugh and often use humor to navigate social interactions.
5. **Dual Nature:** Represented by the twins, Gemini has a dual nature, which can manifest as versatility or inconsistency. They can be both introverted and extroverted, serious and playful, depending on the situation.

6. **Restlessness and Impatience:** Due to their active minds, Gemini can become restless and impatient. They may struggle with boredom and constantly seek new stimuli to keep themselves engaged.

7. **Curiosity and Open-Mindedness:** Gemini is open-minded and curious about different perspectives. They enjoy exploring new ideas and are often willing to consider unconventional viewpoints.

Gemini in Relationships:

- **Romantic Relationships:** In romantic relationships, Gemini is charming, playful, and communicative. They seek intellectual stimulation and enjoy engaging in meaningful conversations with their partners. Their adaptability allows them to connect with a variety of personalities.

- **Friendships:** As friends, Gemini is fun-loving, supportive, and engaging. They enjoy socializing and bringing people together. Their curiosity ensures they are always interested in their friends' lives and experiences.

- **Family:** Within the family, Gemini takes on an inquisitive and communicative role. They enjoy learning from their family members and sharing their own experiences. Their adaptability helps them navigate family dynamics with ease.

- **Career:** In their careers, Gemini excels in roles that require communication, creativity, and adaptability. They thrive in environments that offer variety and intellectual challenges, often excelling in fields such as journalism, marketing, teaching, and public relations.

Best Cannabis Strains for Gemini

Given the dynamic and intellectually driven nature of Gemini, the best cannabis strains for this sign should enhance their natural qualities and provide mental clarity and focus. Strains that promote creativity, energy, and social engagement can help Gemini stay sharp and engaged.

Harlequin: Clear-Headed and Focused

Harlequin is a sativa-dominant strain known for its high CBD content and clear-headed effects. It is an excellent choice for Gemini individuals who seek mental clarity and focus without intense psychoactive effects.

- **Effects:** Harlequin offers a balanced, clear-headed high that enhances focus and concentration. Its high CBD content helps to reduce anxiety and promote mental calmness, making it ideal for tasks requiring precision and clear thinking.
- **Flavor and Aroma:** This strain has an earthy, woody aroma with hints of mango and citrus, contributing to its refreshing profile.
- **Usage:** Harlequin is suitable for daytime use, providing mental clarity and focus without overwhelming psychoactive effects, helping Gemini stay sharp and engaged.

Lemon Haze: Energizing and Uplifting

Lemon Haze is a sativa-dominant strain known for its uplifting and energizing effects. It is perfect for Gemini individuals seeking a boost in energy and creativity.

- **Effects:** Lemon Haze provides a cheerful, energetic high that promotes focus, creativity, and motivation. Its uplifting effects help to reduce stress and enhance productivity, aligning with Gemini's dynamic and intellectually driven nature.
- **Flavor and Aroma:** This strain has a zesty, citrusy aroma with sweet undertones, adding to its refreshing and invigorating profile.
- **Usage:** Lemon Haze is suitable for daytime use, providing a sustained boost in energy and mental sharpness, helping Gemini stay active and engaged.

Green Crack: Energizing and Motivating

Green Crack, despite its controversial name, is a pure sativa strain famed for its sharp, invigorating effects. It is ideal for Gemini individuals needing a substantial energy boost and mental clarity.

- **Effects:** Green Crack delivers a potent cerebral high that enhances focus, energy, and motivation. Its effects are long-lasting and can help combat stress and fatigue, making it an excellent complement to Gemini's need for mental stimulation and social engagement.
- **Flavor and Aroma:** This strain has a tangy, fruity flavor reminiscent of mango, with an earthy undertone that adds to its vibrant profile.
- **Usage:** Green Crack is best used during the day when mental alertness and physical activity are required, helping Gemini tackle tasks with enthusiasm and vigor.

Super Lemon Haze: Creative and Energizing

Super Lemon Haze is a sativa-dominant hybrid known for its uplifting and mood-enhancing effects. It is perfect for Gemini individuals needing an emotional boost and mental clarity.

- **Effects:** Super Lemon Haze delivers a cerebral, euphoric high that enhances mood and energy levels. It helps to reduce stress and anxiety while promoting a positive, optimistic outlook, aligning with Gemini's dynamic and communicative qualities.
- **Flavor and Aroma:** This strain has a citrusy, earthy aroma with hints of sweetness, contributing to its energizing effects.
- **Usage:** Super Lemon Haze is suitable for daytime use, providing a boost in energy and mood without causing sedation, helping Gemini stay sharp and engaged.

Jack Herer: Creative and Euphoric

Named after the famous cannabis activist, Jack Herer is a well-balanced hybrid strain known for its potent, clear-headed effects and ability to enhance creativity and concentration.

- **Effects:** Jack Herer offers a blissful, euphoric high that stimulates both the mind and body. It promotes a sense of well-being and encourages creative thinking, making it a perfect complement to Gemini's need for mental stimulation and social engagement.
- **Flavor and Aroma:** The strain has a distinctive aroma with notes of pine, earth, and citrus, contributing to its refreshing and energizing effects.
- **Usage:** Jack Herer is often used during creative endeavors or social activities, providing a burst of energy and inspiration without overwhelming the senses.

Conclusion

Gemini, the communicator of the zodiac, is defined by their curiosity, adaptability, and intellectual drive. Understanding their core traits can help us appreciate their vibrant and stimulating nature. By integrating specific cannabis strains that promote mental clarity, energy, and creativity, such as Harlequin, Lemon Haze, Green Crack, Super Lemon Haze, and Jack Herer, Gemini individuals can enhance their natural qualities and stay sharp and engaged in their daily lives. These strains offer a natural way to boost focus, reduce stress, and promote overall well-being, empowering Gemini to communicate, learn, and explore with confidence and enthusiasm. Embracing the influence of Gemini can lead to a life filled with intellectual growth, social connections, and endless curiosity.

Check out my Virtual dispensary for all your hemp needs: https://shift.store/sg1fan23477/retail

Chapter 14: Cancer: The Nurturer

Traits of Cancer

Cancer, the fourth sign of the zodiac, is known as the nurturer. Governed by the Moon, the celestial body of emotions and intuition, Cancer embodies the principles of sensitivity, compassion, and protective instincts. As a cardinal water sign, Cancer is deeply connected to their feelings and the well-being of those they love. Understanding the core traits of Cancer can help us appreciate their nurturing and empathetic nature.

Key Traits of Cancer:

1. **Emotional Sensitivity:** Cancer individuals are highly sensitive and attuned to their own emotions as well as the emotions of others. They have a deep capacity for empathy and often feel things intensely.

2. **Nurturing and Compassionate:** Cancer is known for their nurturing nature. They have a strong desire to care for others and provide emotional support, making them compassionate and loving companions.

3. **Protective and Loyal:** Cancer is fiercely protective of their loved ones. They are loyal and devoted, always ready to defend and support those they care about.

4. **Intuitive and Insightful:** Ruled by the Moon, Cancer possesses strong intuition and insight. They can sense underlying emotions and motivations, often knowing things without needing them to be explicitly stated.

5. **Home and Family-Oriented:** Cancer places a high value on home and family. They find comfort in their personal space and often create warm, inviting environments for themselves and their loved ones.

6. **Creative and Imaginative:** Cancer has a rich inner world and a vivid imagination. They often express themselves through creative pursuits such as art, music, and writing.

7. **Moody and Protective:** Due to their emotional sensitivity, Cancer can be prone to mood swings. They may retreat into their shell when feeling overwhelmed or threatened but emerge stronger and more resilient.

Cancer in Relationships:

- **Romantic Relationships:** In romantic relationships, Cancer is affectionate, devoted, and deeply loving. They seek emotional connection and stability with their partners, often creating a nurturing and supportive environment. Their partners can expect unconditional love and care.

- **Friendships:** As friends, Cancer is loyal, empathetic, and supportive. They are excellent listeners and provide a shoulder to lean on in times of need. Their nurturing nature makes them cherished friends who are always there for those they care about.

- **Family:** Within the family, Cancer takes on a nurturing and protective role. They value family traditions and work hard to create a loving and secure home. Their emotional sensitivity helps them understand and connect with family members on a deep level.

- **Career:** In their careers, Cancer excels in roles that require empathy, intuition, and creativity. They are often found in professions related to caregiving, counseling, the arts, and hospitality, where they can use their nurturing instincts and emotional intelligence.

Best Cannabis Strains for Cancer

Given the emotional and nurturing nature of Cancer, the best cannabis strains for this sign should enhance their natural qualities and provide relaxation, emotional balance, and creativity. Strains that promote relaxation, reduce stress, and enhance emotional well-being can help Cancer find comfort and maintain their nurturing spirit.

Blue Dream: Relaxing and Uplifting

Blue Dream is a hybrid strain celebrated for its balanced effects that provide both relaxation and mental invigoration. It is an excellent choice for Cancer individuals who seek to enhance creativity and emotional balance.

- **Effects:** Blue Dream offers a gentle, euphoric high that helps to calm the mind and uplift the spirit. It provides a sense of mental clarity and relaxation without sedation, making it ideal for managing stress and enhancing mood.
- **Flavor and Aroma:** This strain has a sweet, berry-like aroma with earthy undertones, contributing to its soothing effects.
- **Usage:** Blue Dream is suitable for any time of day, providing emotional stability and a positive mindset without overwhelming the senses.

OG Kush: Calming and Grounding

OG Kush is a hybrid strain known for its potent relaxing effects and ability to provide a sense of grounding. It is ideal for those seeking to reduce stress and enhance focus.

- **Effects:** OG Kush offers a calming, euphoric high that helps to reduce stress and promote relaxation. Its grounding effects can enhance focus and provide a sense of stability, aligning well with Cancer's nurturing and protective nature.
- **Flavor and Aroma:** This strain has a complex aroma with notes of earth, pine, and citrus, contributing to its soothing and grounding properties.
- **Usage:** OG Kush is suitable for evening use or during times of high stress, helping Cancer unwind and regain emotional balance.

Northern Lights: Relaxing and Calming

Northern Lights is a classic indica strain known for its deeply relaxing and calming effects. It is highly effective for those needing to unwind and achieve emotional tranquility.

- **Effects:** Northern Lights delivers a potent, body-focused high that promotes relaxation and sleep. Its calming effects help to alleviate stress, anxiety, and emotional tension, making it a perfect strain for grounding and focus.
- **Flavor and Aroma:** This strain has a sweet, earthy aroma with hints of pine and spice, adding to its comforting profile.
- **Usage:** Northern Lights is best used in the evening or before bed to help relax the body and mind, promoting restful sleep and emotional peace.

Lavender: Tranquil and Soothing

Lavender is an indica-dominant strain known for its strong calming and sedative effects. It is ideal for those seeking deep relaxation and enhanced spiritual experiences.

- **Effects:** Lavender provides a heavy, tranquilizing high that eases the mind and body into a state of deep relaxation. Its calming effects help to quiet the mind and promote a sense of peace, making it perfect for meditation and emotional healing.
- **Flavor and Aroma:** This strain has a floral, lavender-like aroma with hints of herbs and spices, enhancing its soothing properties.
- **Usage:** Lavender is best used in the evening or during spiritual practices to promote relaxation, inner peace, and emotional balance.

Granddaddy Purple: Relaxing and Comforting

Granddaddy Purple (GDP) is an indica strain known for its deeply relaxing and soothing effects. It is an excellent choice for Cancer individuals who seek comfort and stress relief.

- **Effects:** Granddaddy Purple offers a calming, euphoric high that promotes relaxation and sleep. Its powerful effects help to reduce stress and anxiety, making it perfect for Cancer's love of comfort and relaxation.
- **Flavor and Aroma:** This strain has a sweet, grape-like aroma with earthy undertones, contributing to its comforting and enjoyable experience.
- **Usage:** Granddaddy Purple is best used in the evening or before bed to help Cancer unwind and achieve a deep, restful sleep.

Conclusion

Cancer, the nurturer of the zodiac, is defined by their emotional sensitivity, nurturing instincts, and deep compassion. Understanding their core traits can help us appreciate their caring and empathetic nature. By integrating specific cannabis strains that promote relaxation, emotional balance, and creativity, such as Blue Dream, OG Kush, Northern Lights, Lavender, and Granddaddy Purple, Cancer individuals can enhance their natural qualities and find comfort and relaxation in their daily lives. These strains offer a natural way to boost relaxation, reduce stress, and promote overall well-being, empowering Cancer to nurture, protect, and care for themselves and their loved ones with confidence and compassion. Embracing the influence of Cancer can lead to a life filled with emotional depth, creative expression, and meaningful connections.

Check out my Virtual dispensary for all your hemp needs: https://shift.store/sg1fan23477/retail

Chapter 15: Leo: The Leader

Traits of Leo

Leo, the fifth sign of the zodiac, is known as the leader. Governed by the Sun, the center of our solar system, Leo embodies the principles of creativity, confidence, and charisma. As a fixed fire sign, Leo is passionate, energetic, and always ready to take center stage. Understanding the core traits of Leo can help us appreciate their vibrant, ambitious, and generous nature.

Key Traits of Leo:

1. **Confidence and Charisma:** Leo individuals are naturally confident and charismatic. They have a strong presence and are often the center of attention in any social setting.
2. **Creativity and Self-Expression:** Leo is highly creative and expressive. They enjoy artistic pursuits and often have a flair for drama and performance.
3. **Generosity and Warmth:** Leo is known for their generosity and warmth. They are kind-hearted and enjoy sharing their abundance with others, often going out of their way to help friends and family.
4. **Leadership and Ambition:** Leo possesses strong leadership qualities and ambition. They are natural leaders who inspire and motivate others, often taking charge in group settings.
5. **Passion and Enthusiasm:** Leo is passionate and enthusiastic about life. They approach their goals with energy and determination, often inspiring others with their zest for life.
6. **Loyalty and Protectiveness:** Leo is fiercely loyal and protective of their loved ones. They value loyalty in return and are always ready to defend and support those they care about.
7. **Pride and Stubbornness:** Due to their strong sense of self, Leo can sometimes be prideful and stubborn. They may struggle with admitting when they are wrong or accepting criticism.

Leo in Relationships:

- **Romantic Relationships:** In romantic relationships, Leo is affectionate, passionate, and devoted. They seek partners who can match their energy and enthusiasm, often creating a dynamic and exciting relationship. Their partners can expect grand gestures of love and unwavering loyalty.
- **Friendships:** As friends, Leo is generous, supportive, and fun-loving. They enjoy socializing and bringing people together, often organizing gatherings and events. Their friends can rely on their loyalty and enjoy their vibrant presence.
- **Family:** Within the family, Leo takes on a protective and nurturing role. They value family traditions and work hard to create a loving and secure environment. Their warmth and generosity often make them the heart of the family.
- **Career:** In their careers, Leo excels in roles that require leadership, creativity, and public engagement. They are often found in professions related to the arts, entertainment, management, and public relations, where they can shine and inspire others.

Best Cannabis Strains for Leo

Given the dynamic and energetic nature of Leo, the best cannabis strains for this sign should enhance their natural qualities and provide energy, creativity, and relaxation. Strains that promote focus, creativity, and stress relief can help Leo stay motivated and balanced.

Pineapple Express: Energizing and Creative

Pineapple Express is a hybrid strain known for its balanced effects, offering both mental stimulation and physical relaxation. It is a favorite for Leo individuals who seek a harmonious blend of energy and calmness.

- **Effects:** Pineapple Express provides a mild, euphoric high that promotes happiness and creativity. It enhances focus and productivity while also offering a subtle body relaxation, making it a versatile strain that resonates with Leo's vibrant and dynamic nature.

- **Flavor and Aroma:** This strain has a delightful tropical aroma with hints of pineapple and citrus, contributing to its refreshing and enjoyable effects.
- **Usage:** Pineapple Express is suitable for any time of day, particularly when a balanced approach to energy and relaxation is desired, helping Leo stay motivated and grounded.

Sour Diesel: Uplifting and Euphoric

Sour Diesel is a sativa-dominant strain renowned for its fast-acting, energizing effects. It is a popular choice for Leo individuals who seek to enhance vitality and mental clarity.

- **Effects:** Sour Diesel provides an uplifting and euphoric high, making it ideal for combating fatigue and promoting a positive mindset. It can help spark creativity and motivation, aligning well with Leo's need for action and excitement.
- **Flavor and Aroma:** This strain has a pungent diesel-like aroma with hints of citrus and earthiness, adding to its invigorating profile.
- **Usage:** Sour Diesel is suitable for daytime use, helping Leo stay active, focused, and inspired throughout the day.

Jack Herer: Creative and Euphoric

Named after the famous cannabis activist, Jack Herer is a well-balanced hybrid strain known for its potent, clear-headed effects and ability to enhance creativity and concentration.

- **Effects:** Jack Herer offers a blissful, euphoric high that stimulates both the mind and body. It promotes a sense of well-being and encourages creative thinking, making it a perfect complement to Leo's need for mental stimulation and social engagement.

- **Flavor and Aroma:** The strain has a distinctive aroma with notes of pine, earth, and citrus, contributing to its refreshing and energizing effects.
- **Usage:** Jack Herer is often used during creative endeavors or social activities, providing a burst of energy and inspiration without overwhelming the senses.

Lemon Haze: Energizing and Uplifting

Lemon Haze is a sativa-dominant strain known for its uplifting and energizing effects. It is perfect for Leo individuals seeking a boost in energy and creativity.

- **Effects:** Lemon Haze provides a cheerful, energetic high that promotes focus, creativity, and motivation. Its uplifting effects help to reduce stress and enhance productivity, aligning with Leo's dynamic and creative nature.
- **Flavor and Aroma:** This strain has a zesty, citrusy aroma with sweet undertones, adding to its refreshing and invigorating profile.
- **Usage:** Lemon Haze is suitable for daytime use, providing a sustained boost in energy and mental sharpness, helping Leo stay active and engaged.

Blue Dream: Relaxing and Uplifting

Blue Dream is a hybrid strain celebrated for its balanced effects that provide both relaxation and mental invigoration. It is an excellent choice for Leo individuals who seek to enhance creativity and stress relief during transformational periods.

- **Effects:** Blue Dream offers a gentle, euphoric high that helps to calm the mind and uplift the spirit. It provides a sense of mental

clarity and relaxation without sedation, making it ideal for creative projects and personal growth.

- **Flavor and Aroma:** This strain has a sweet, berry-like aroma with earthy undertones, contributing to its soothing effects.
- **Usage:** Blue Dream is suitable for any time of day, providing emotional stability and a positive mindset without overwhelming the senses.

Conclusion

Leo, the leader of the zodiac, is defined by their confidence, creativity, and charisma. Understanding their core traits can help us appreciate their vibrant and ambitious nature. By integrating specific cannabis strains that promote energy, creativity, and relaxation, such as Pineapple Express, Sour Diesel, Jack Herer, Lemon Haze, and Blue Dream, Leo individuals can enhance their natural qualities and stay motivated and balanced in their daily lives. These strains offer a natural way to boost focus, reduce stress, and promote overall well-being, empowering Leo to lead, create, and inspire with confidence and enthusiasm. Embracing the influence of Leo can lead to a life filled with excitement, growth, and endless possibilities.

Check out my Virtual dispensary for all your hemp needs: https://shift.store/sg1fan23477/retail

Chapter 16: Virgo: The Analyst

Traits of Virgo

Virgo, the sixth sign of the zodiac, is known as the analyst. Governed by Mercury, the planet of communication and intellect, Virgo embodies the principles of precision, practicality, and meticulousness. As a mutable earth sign, Virgo is adaptable, grounded, and highly analytical. Understanding the core traits of Virgo can help us appreciate their detail-oriented, helpful, and intellectually sharp nature.

Key Traits of Virgo:

1. **Attention to Detail:** Virgo individuals are known for their keen attention to detail. They have an exceptional ability to notice the finer points and ensure that everything is perfect.

2. **Practicality and Efficiency:** Virgo is highly practical and efficient. They approach tasks with a methodical mindset and are always looking for the most effective and logical way to achieve their goals.

3. **Analytical and Intellectual:** Virgo possesses strong analytical and intellectual abilities. They enjoy solving problems, organizing information, and understanding how things work.

4. **Reliability and Responsibility:** Virgo is reliable and responsible. They take their duties seriously and are always there to support others and ensure that tasks are completed accurately.

5. **Modesty and Humility:** Despite their many talents, Virgo is often modest and humble. They prefer to work behind the scenes and do not seek the spotlight.

6. **Health and Wellness Conscious:** Virgo places a high value on health and wellness. They are often knowledgeable about nutrition, fitness, and holistic practices, striving to maintain a healthy lifestyle.

7. **Service-Oriented:** Virgo has a strong desire to help others. They are service-oriented and find fulfillment in making a positive difference in the lives of those around them.

Virgo in Relationships:

- **Romantic Relationships:** In romantic relationships, Virgo is attentive, loyal, and supportive. They seek a partner who appreciates their practicality and intellect. Their love is often expressed through acts of service and thoughtful gestures.
- **Friendships:** As friends, Virgo is dependable, trustworthy, and helpful. They are always ready to offer practical advice and support. Their friends can count on them for their reliability and attention to detail.
- **Family:** Within the family, Virgo takes on a nurturing and responsible role. They are often the caretakers, ensuring that everything runs smoothly and that family members are well taken care of.
- **Career:** In their careers, Virgo excels in roles that require precision, organization, and analytical thinking. They are often found in professions related to healthcare, research, accounting, and administration, where they can apply their skills and make a meaningful impact.

Best Cannabis Strains for Virgo

Given the analytical and practical nature of Virgo, the best cannabis strains for this sign should enhance their natural qualities and provide mental clarity, focus, and relaxation. Strains that promote mental clarity, reduce stress, and enhance focus can help Virgo maintain their productivity and well-being.

ACDC: Clear-Headed and Relaxing

ACDC is a hybrid strain renowned for its high CBD content and minimal psychoactive effects. It is perfect for Virgo individuals seeking relaxation and mental clarity without the high.

- **Effects:** ACDC provides a relaxing, clear-headed high that enhances focus and reduces stress. Its high CBD content helps to calm the mind and body, making it suitable for tasks requiring mental clarity and composure.
- **Flavor and Aroma:** This strain has a sweet, earthy aroma with hints of citrus and pine, adding to its calming effects.
- **Usage:** ACDC is best used during the day when mental alertness and relaxation are needed, providing a clear mind and calm demeanor.

Harlequin: Clear-Headed and Focused

Harlequin is a sativa-dominant strain known for its high CBD content and clear-headed effects. It is an excellent choice for Virgo individuals who seek mental clarity and focus without intense psychoactive effects.

- **Effects:** Harlequin offers a balanced, clear-headed high that enhances focus and concentration. Its high CBD content helps to reduce anxiety and promote mental calmness, making it ideal for tasks requiring precision and clear thinking.
- **Flavor and Aroma:** This strain has an earthy, woody aroma with hints of mango and citrus, contributing to its refreshing profile.
- **Usage:** Harlequin is suitable for daytime use, providing mental clarity and focus without overwhelming psychoactive effects, helping Virgo stay sharp and engaged.

Sour Tsunami: Balanced and Clear-Headed

Sour Tsunami is a hybrid strain known for its high CBD content and balanced effects. It is ideal for those seeking clear-headedness and relaxation.

- **Effects:** Sour Tsunami offers a balanced high that enhances focus and mental clarity. Its high CBD content helps to reduce stress and anxiety, promoting a calm and clear mind.
- **Flavor and Aroma:** This strain has a sour, earthy aroma with hints of citrus and diesel, contributing to its invigorating profile.
- **Usage:** Sour Tsunami is suitable for any time of day, providing mental clarity and relaxation without intense psychoactive effects.

Cannatonic: Relaxing and Uplifting

Cannatonic is a hybrid strain known for its balanced THC and CBD content, providing mild psychoactive effects and clear-headed relaxation.

- **Effects:** Cannatonic offers a relaxing, uplifting high that promotes mental clarity and focus. Its balanced THC and CBD content helps to reduce stress and enhance cognitive function without overwhelming euphoria.
- **Flavor and Aroma:** This strain has a mild, earthy aroma with hints of pine and citrus, contributing to its soothing effects.
- **Usage:** Cannatonic is suitable for daytime use, providing a balanced approach to relaxation and mental clarity.

Pennywise: Focused and Relaxing

Pennywise is an indica-dominant strain known for its high CBD content and minimal psychoactive effects. It is perfect for those seeking mental clarity and focus.

- **Effects:** Pennywise provides a clear-headed, focused high that enhances cognitive function and reduces stress. Its high CBD content helps to calm the mind and promote mental clarity without intense psychoactive effects.
- **Flavor and Aroma:** This strain has an earthy, citrus aroma with hints of sweetness, adding to its refreshing profile.

- **Usage:** Pennywise is best used during the day when mental alertness and relaxation are needed, providing a clear mind and focused demeanor.

Conclusion

Virgo, the analyst of the zodiac, is defined by their precision, practicality, and analytical prowess. Understanding their core traits can help us appreciate their detail-oriented and service-oriented nature. By integrating specific cannabis strains that promote mental clarity, focus, and relaxation, such as ACDC, Harlequin, Sour Tsunami, Cannatonic, and Pennywise, Virgo individuals can enhance their natural qualities and maintain their productivity and well-being. These strains offer a natural way to boost focus, reduce stress, and promote overall well-being, empowering Virgo to analyze, organize, and excel with confidence and efficiency. Embracing the influence of Virgo can lead to a life filled with intellectual growth, practical achievements, and meaningful contributions to the well-being of others.

Check out my Virtual dispensary for all your hemp needs: https://shift.store/sg1fan23477/retail

Chapter 17: Libra: The Harmonizer
Traits of Libra

Libra, the seventh sign of the zodiac, is known as the harmonizer. Governed by Venus, the planet of love, beauty, and balance, Libra embodies the principles of harmony, fairness, and sociability. As a cardinal air sign, Libra is diplomatic, charming, and naturally attuned to the needs of others. Understanding the core traits of Libra can help us appreciate their graceful, balanced, and justice-oriented nature.

Key Traits of Libra:

1. **Balance and Harmony:** Libra individuals are driven by a desire for balance and harmony in all aspects of life. They strive to create equilibrium in their relationships, environment, and personal well-being.
2. **Diplomatic and Fair-Minded:** Libra is naturally diplomatic and fair-minded. They have a strong sense of justice and are skilled at mediating conflicts and finding equitable solutions.
3. **Sociable and Charming:** Libra is highly sociable and charming. They enjoy interacting with others and are often the life of social gatherings. Their charm and tact make them excellent communicators.
4. **Appreciation for Beauty:** Ruled by Venus, Libra has a keen appreciation for beauty and aesthetics. They are drawn to art, design, and all forms of creative expression.
5. **Romantic and Idealistic:** Libra is romantic and idealistic, often envisioning perfect relationships and striving to achieve them. They seek deep, meaningful connections and value partnership.

6. **Indecisive and Avoidant:** Due to their desire for balance, Libra can sometimes struggle with indecisiveness and a tendency to avoid conflict. They may take time to weigh all options before making decisions.

7. **Cooperative and Team-Oriented:** Libra thrives in cooperative and team-oriented environments. They enjoy working with others towards common goals and are skilled at fostering collaboration.

Libra in Relationships:

- **Romantic Relationships:** In romantic relationships, Libra is affectionate, romantic, and devoted. They seek partners who can appreciate their need for harmony and balance. Their partners can expect a relationship filled with love, beauty, and mutual respect.
- **Friendships:** As friends, Libra is loyal, supportive, and fun-loving. They enjoy socializing and bringing people together. Their friends can rely on their diplomatic skills and enjoy their warm, engaging presence.
- **Family:** Within the family, Libra takes on a nurturing and supportive role. They value family harmony and work hard to create a peaceful and loving environment. Their sense of fairness helps them navigate family dynamics with ease.
- **Career:** In their careers, Libra excels in roles that require diplomacy, creativity, and collaboration. They are often found in professions related to law, art, design, public relations, and counseling, where they can use their skills to foster harmony and create beauty.

Best Cannabis Strains for Libra

Given the harmonious and sociable nature of Libra, the best cannabis strains for this sign should enhance their natural qualities and provide relaxation, creativity, and social engagement. Strains that promote relaxation, reduce stress, and enhance mood can help Libra maintain their balance and well-being.

Cherry Pie: Relaxing and Uplifting

Cherry Pie is a hybrid strain known for its balanced effects and sweet, fruity flavor. It is perfect for Libra individuals seeking relaxation and a sense of well-being.

- **Effects:** Cherry Pie offers a calming, blissful high that helps to reduce stress and promote relaxation. Its balanced effects make it ideal for enhancing feelings of love and connection, fostering a warm and affectionate atmosphere.
- **Flavor and Aroma:** This strain has a sweet, cherry-like aroma with earthy undertones, contributing to its soothing and enjoyable experience.
- **Usage:** Cherry Pie is suitable for any time of day, providing relaxation and a positive mood that enhances romantic and social interactions.

Strawberry Cough: Uplifting and Euphoric

Strawberry Cough is a sativa-dominant strain known for its uplifting and euphoric effects. It is an excellent choice for Libra individuals who seek to enhance their mood and social engagement.

- **Effects:** Strawberry Cough provides a cerebral, uplifting high that promotes feelings of happiness and well-being. Its euphoric effects can enhance social interactions and create a loving, relaxed environment.
- **Flavor and Aroma:** This strain has a sweet, strawberry-like aroma with hints of spice, adding to its delightful sensory experience.
- **Usage:** Strawberry Cough is suitable for daytime use, providing a boost in mood and energy that enhances social and romantic interactions.

Blue Dream: Creative and Relaxing

Blue Dream is a hybrid strain celebrated for its balanced effects that provide both relaxation and mental invigoration. It is an excellent choice for Libra individuals who seek to enhance creativity and stress relief.

- **Effects:** Blue Dream offers a gentle, euphoric high that helps to calm the mind and uplift the spirit. It provides a sense of mental clarity and relaxation without sedation, making it ideal for managing stress and enhancing mood.
- **Flavor and Aroma:** This strain has a sweet, berry-like aroma with earthy undertones, contributing to its soothing effects.
- **Usage:** Blue Dream is suitable for any time of day, providing emotional stability and a positive mindset without overwhelming the senses.

Lemon Haze: Energizing and Uplifting

Lemon Haze is a sativa-dominant strain known for its uplifting and energizing effects. It is perfect for Libra individuals seeking a boost in energy and creativity.

- **Effects:** Lemon Haze provides a cheerful, energetic high that promotes focus, creativity, and motivation. Its uplifting effects help to reduce stress and enhance productivity, aligning with Libra's dynamic and creative nature.
- **Flavor and Aroma:** This strain has a zesty, citrusy aroma with sweet undertones, adding to its refreshing and invigorating profile.
- **Usage:** Lemon Haze is suitable for daytime use, providing a sustained boost in energy and mental sharpness, helping Libra stay active and engaged.

OG Kush: Calming and Grounding

OG Kush is a hybrid strain known for its potent relaxing effects and ability to provide a sense of grounding. It is ideal for those seeking to reduce stress and enhance focus.

- **Effects:** OG Kush offers a calming, euphoric high that helps to reduce stress and promote relaxation. Its grounding effects can enhance focus and provide a sense of stability, aligning well with Libra's need for balance and harmony.
- **Flavor and Aroma:** This strain has a complex aroma with notes of earth, pine, and citrus, contributing to its soothing and grounding properties.
- **Usage:** OG Kush is suitable for evening use or during times of high stress, helping Libra unwind and regain emotional balance.

Conclusion

Libra, the harmonizer of the zodiac, is defined by their desire for balance, fairness, and social harmony. Understanding their core traits can help us appreciate their diplomatic and charming nature. By integrating specific cannabis strains that promote relaxation, creativity, and social engagement, such as Cherry Pie, Strawberry Cough, Blue Dream, Lemon Haze, and OG Kush, Libra individuals can enhance their natural qualities and maintain their balance and well-being. These strains offer a natural way to boost focus, reduce stress, and promote overall well-being, empowering Libra to foster harmony, create beauty, and build meaningful connections with others. Embracing the influence of Libra can lead to a life filled with love, beauty, and harmonious relationships.

Check out my Virtual dispensary for all your hemp needs: https://shift.store/sg1fan23477/retail

Chapter 18: Scorpio: The Transformer
Traits of Scorpio

Scorpio, the eighth sign of the zodiac, is known as the transformer. Governed by Pluto, the planet of transformation and power, and Mars, the planet of action and desire, Scorpio embodies the principles of intensity, depth, and regeneration. As a fixed water sign, Scorpio is deeply emotional, mysterious, and fiercely determined. Understanding the core traits of Scorpio can help us appreciate their transformative, passionate, and resilient nature.

Key Traits of Scorpio:

1. **Intensity and Passion:** Scorpio individuals are known for their intense and passionate nature. They approach life with a fervor that is unmatched, fully committing to everything they do.
2. **Emotional Depth:** Scorpio has a profound emotional depth. They experience emotions intensely and are deeply connected to their inner selves and the feelings of others.
3. **Mystery and Secrecy:** Scorpio is naturally mysterious and secretive. They tend to keep their true thoughts and feelings hidden, revealing them only to those they trust deeply.
4. **Determination and Willpower:** Scorpio possesses immense determination and willpower. Once they set their mind on something, they pursue it relentlessly until they achieve their goals.
5. **Transformative and Regenerative:** Scorpio is the sign of transformation and regeneration. They have the ability to rise from the ashes, constantly reinventing themselves and evolving through life's challenges.
6. **Insightfulness and Intuition:** Scorpio is highly intuitive and insightful. They have a natural ability to see beneath the surface and understand hidden truths and motivations.

7. **Loyalty and Protection:** Scorpio is fiercely loyal and protective of their loved ones. They form deep bonds and are always ready to defend and support those they care about.

Scorpio in Relationships:

- **Romantic Relationships:** In romantic relationships, Scorpio is passionate, loyal, and deeply committed. They seek intense, transformative connections with their partners and value emotional depth and honesty. Their partners can expect a relationship filled with intensity, loyalty, and profound emotional experiences.
- **Friendships:** As friends, Scorpio is loyal, supportive, and protective. They form deep, lasting friendships and are always there to offer insightful advice and support. Their friends can rely on their unwavering loyalty and trustworthiness.
- **Family:** Within the family, Scorpio takes on a protective and nurturing role. They value family bonds and work hard to create a secure and supportive environment. Their emotional depth helps them connect deeply with family members.
- **Career:** In their careers, Scorpio excels in roles that require intensity, focus, and insight. They are often found in professions related to psychology, research, investigation, and healing, where they can use their transformative abilities and deep understanding of human nature.

Best Cannabis Strains for Scorpio

Given the intense and transformative nature of Scorpio, the best cannabis strains for this sign should enhance their natural qualities and provide deep relaxation, mental clarity, and emotional balance. Strains that promote introspection, reduce stress, and enhance focus can help Scorpio maintain their resilience and well-being.

Trainwreck: Energizing and Mind-Expanding

Trainwreck is a sativa-dominant hybrid strain known for its potent, mind-expanding effects and ability to promote creativity and introspection. It is perfect for Scorpio individuals seeking profound transformation and mental clarity.

- **Effects:** Trainwreck provides a strong, cerebral high that enhances focus, creativity, and motivation. Its intense effects help to reduce stress and promote a sense of mental clarity, making it ideal for deep personal transformation and emotional healing.
- **Flavor and Aroma:** This strain has a pungent, earthy aroma with hints of pine and citrus, contributing to its invigorating and transformative profile.
- **Usage:** Trainwreck is suitable for daytime use, providing a sustained boost in energy and mental sharpness, helping Scorpio engage in introspection and personal growth.

Gorilla Glue: Intense and Transformative

Gorilla Glue, also known as GG4, is a potent hybrid strain known for its powerful effects and ability to promote deep relaxation and introspection. It is ideal for those seeking profound transformation and emotional release.

- **Effects:** Gorilla Glue delivers a heavy, euphoric high that promotes deep relaxation and mental clarity. Its intense effects help to alleviate stress and anxiety, making it perfect for deep introspection and personal transformation.
- **Flavor and Aroma:** This strain has a pungent, earthy aroma with hints of pine and sour notes, contributing to its grounding and transformative properties.
- **Usage:** Gorilla Glue is best used in the evening or during periods of high stress, helping individuals to unwind and engage in deep introspection and emotional release.

Northern Lights: Relaxing and Calming

Northern Lights is a classic indica strain known for its deeply relaxing and calming effects. It is highly effective for those needing to unwind and achieve emotional tranquility.

- **Effects:** Northern Lights delivers a potent, body-focused high that promotes relaxation and sleep. Its calming effects help to alleviate stress, anxiety, and emotional tension, making it a perfect strain for grounding and focus.
- **Flavor and Aroma:** This strain has a sweet, earthy aroma with hints of pine and spice, adding to its comforting profile.
- **Usage:** Northern Lights is best used in the evening or before bed to help relax the body and mind, promoting restful sleep and emotional peace.

Blue Dream: Creative and Uplifting

Blue Dream is a hybrid strain celebrated for its balanced effects that provide both relaxation and mental invigoration. It is an excellent choice for Scorpio individuals who seek to enhance creativity and stress relief during transformational periods.

- **Effects:** Blue Dream offers a gentle, euphoric high that helps to calm the mind and uplift the spirit. It provides a sense of mental clarity and relaxation without sedation, making it ideal for creative projects and personal growth.
- **Flavor and Aroma:** This strain has a sweet, berry-like aroma with earthy undertones, contributing to its soothing effects.
- **Usage:** Blue Dream is suitable for any time of day, providing emotional stability and a positive mindset without overwhelming the senses, supporting deep transformation and healing.

Lavender: Tranquil and Soothing

Lavender is an indica-dominant strain known for its strong calming and sedative effects. It is ideal for those seeking deep relaxation and enhanced spiritual experiences.

- **Effects:** Lavender provides a heavy, tranquilizing high that eases the mind and body into a state of deep relaxation. Its calming effects help to quiet the mind and promote a sense of peace, making it perfect for meditation and emotional healing.
- **Flavor and Aroma:** This strain has a floral, lavender-like aroma with hints of herbs and spices, enhancing its soothing properties.
- **Usage:** Lavender is best used in the evening or during spiritual practices to promote relaxation, inner peace, and emotional balance.

Conclusion

Scorpio, the transformer of the zodiac, is defined by their intensity, emotional depth, and transformative power. Understanding their core traits can help us appreciate their passionate and resilient nature. By integrating specific cannabis strains that promote relaxation, mental clarity, and emotional balance, such as Trainwreck, Gorilla Glue, Northern Lights, Blue Dream, and Lavender, Scorpio individuals can enhance their natural qualities and maintain their resilience and well-being. These strains offer a natural way to boost focus, reduce stress, and promote overall well-being, empowering Scorpio to navigate life's challenges, transform, and evolve with confidence and strength. Embracing the influence of Scorpio can lead to a life filled with profound transformation, personal growth, and deep emotional connections.

Check out my Virtual dispensary for all your hemp needs: https://shift.store/sg1fan23477/retail

Chapter 19: Sagittarius: The Explorer
Traits of Sagittarius

Sagittarius, the ninth sign of the zodiac, is known as the explorer. Governed by Jupiter, the planet of expansion, optimism, and wisdom, Sagittarius embodies the principles of adventure, freedom, and philosophical inquiry. As a mutable fire sign, Sagittarius is dynamic, enthusiastic, and always seeking new experiences and knowledge. Understanding the core traits of Sagittarius can help us appreciate their adventurous, optimistic, and intellectually curious nature.

Key Traits of Sagittarius:

1. **Adventurous and Free-Spirited:** Sagittarius individuals are natural adventurers. They have a strong desire to explore new places, ideas, and experiences. Their free-spirited nature drives them to seek out the unknown and embrace new challenges.

2. **Optimistic and Enthusiastic:** Sagittarius is inherently optimistic and enthusiastic. They approach life with a positive attitude and a sense of excitement, often inspiring others with their boundless energy and zest for life.

3. **Intellectual and Philosophical:** Sagittarius has a deep love for learning and philosophical inquiry. They are intellectually curious and enjoy exploring different belief systems, cultures, and perspectives.

4. **Honest and Direct:** Sagittarius is known for their honesty and directness. They value truth and transparency and are not afraid to speak their mind, sometimes with bluntness.

5. **Independent and Freedom-Loving:** Sagittarius values their independence and freedom. They resist constraints and seek opportunities that allow them to express their individuality and pursue their passions.

6. **Generous and Open-Minded:** Sagittarius is generous and open-minded. They are willing to embrace new ideas and experiences, often sharing their knowledge and resources with others.

7. **Restless and Impatient:** Due to their love for adventure and new experiences, Sagittarius can sometimes be restless and impatient. They may struggle with routine and boredom, constantly seeking new stimuli to keep themselves engaged.

Sagittarius in Relationships:

- **Romantic Relationships:** In romantic relationships, Sagittarius is adventurous, passionate, and open-minded. They seek partners who can share in their love for exploration and intellectual growth. Their partners can expect a relationship filled with excitement, honesty, and mutual growth.

- **Friendships:** As friends, Sagittarius is loyal, supportive, and fun-loving. They enjoy socializing and bringing people together, often planning adventurous outings and activities. Their friends can rely on their optimism and willingness to explore new ideas and experiences.

- **Family:** Within the family, Sagittarius takes on a nurturing and supportive role. They value family bonds and work hard to create a loving and open environment. Their sense of adventure often inspires family members to embrace new experiences.

- **Career:** In their careers, Sagittarius excels in roles that require creativity, exploration, and intellectual engagement. They are often found in professions related to travel, education, philosophy, and the arts, where they can use their adventurous spirit and love for learning.

Best Cannabis Strains for Sagittarius
Given the adventurous and intellectually curious nature of Sagittarius, the best cannabis strains for this sign should enhance their natural

qualities and provide energy, creativity, and relaxation. Strains that promote focus, creativity, and mental clarity can help Sagittarius stay motivated and balanced while exploring new ideas and experiences.

Super Lemon Haze: Energizing and Uplifting

Super Lemon Haze is a sativa-dominant hybrid known for its uplifting and energizing effects. It is perfect for Sagittarius individuals seeking a boost in energy and creativity.

- **Effects:** Super Lemon Haze provides a cheerful, energetic high that promotes focus, creativity, and motivation. Its uplifting effects help to reduce stress and enhance productivity, aligning with Sagittarius's dynamic and adventurous nature.
- **Flavor and Aroma:** This strain has a zesty, citrusy aroma with sweet undertones, adding to its refreshing and invigorating profile.
- **Usage:** Super Lemon Haze is suitable for daytime use, providing a sustained boost in energy and mental sharpness, helping Sagittarius stay active and engaged.

Blue Dream: Creative and Uplifting

Blue Dream is a hybrid strain celebrated for its balanced effects that provide both relaxation and mental invigoration. It is an excellent choice for Sagittarius individuals who seek to enhance creativity and stress relief during their explorations.

- **Effects:** Blue Dream offers a gentle, euphoric high that helps to calm the mind and uplift the spirit. It provides a sense of mental clarity and relaxation without sedation, making it ideal for creative projects and intellectual pursuits.
- **Flavor and Aroma:** This strain has a sweet, berry-like aroma with earthy undertones, contributing to its soothing effects.

- **Usage:** Blue Dream is suitable for any time of day, providing emotional stability and a positive mindset without overwhelming the senses, supporting Sagittarius's love for learning and exploration.

Green Crack: Energizing and Motivating

Green Crack, despite its controversial name, is a pure sativa strain famed for its sharp, invigorating effects. It is ideal for Sagittarius individuals needing a substantial energy boost and mental clarity.

- **Effects:** Green Crack delivers a potent cerebral high that enhances focus, energy, and motivation. Its effects are long-lasting and can help combat stress and fatigue, making it an excellent complement to Sagittarius's need for adventure and intellectual engagement.
- **Flavor and Aroma:** This strain has a tangy, fruity flavor reminiscent of mango, with an earthy undertone that adds to its vibrant profile.
- **Usage:** Green Crack is best used during the day when mental alertness and physical activity are required, helping Sagittarius tackle tasks with enthusiasm and vigor.

Amnesia Haze: Uplifting and Creative

Amnesia Haze is a sativa-dominant strain known for its uplifting and mood-enhancing effects. It is perfect for Sagittarius individuals needing an emotional boost and mental clarity.

- **Effects:** Amnesia Haze delivers a cerebral, euphoric high that enhances mood and energy levels. It helps to reduce stress and anxiety while promoting a positive, optimistic outlook, aligning with Sagittarius's dynamic and optimistic qualities.
- **Flavor and Aroma:** This strain has a citrusy, earthy aroma with hints of sweetness, contributing to its uplifting effects.

- **Usage:** Amnesia Haze is suitable for daytime use, providing a boost in energy and mood without causing sedation, helping Sagittarius stay sharp and engaged.

Jack Herer: Creative and Euphoric

Named after the famous cannabis activist, Jack Herer is a well-balanced hybrid strain known for its potent, clear-headed effects and ability to enhance creativity and concentration.

- **Effects:** Jack Herer offers a blissful, euphoric high that stimulates both the mind and body. It promotes a sense of well-being and encourages creative thinking, making it a perfect complement to Sagittarius's need for mental stimulation and intellectual exploration.
- **Flavor and Aroma:** The strain has a distinctive aroma with notes of pine, earth, and citrus, contributing to its refreshing and energizing effects.
- **Usage:** Jack Herer is often used during creative endeavors or social activities, providing a burst of energy and inspiration without overwhelming the senses.

Conclusion

Sagittarius, the explorer of the zodiac, is defined by their adventurous spirit, intellectual curiosity, and boundless optimism. Understanding their core traits can help us appreciate their dynamic and enthusiastic nature. By integrating specific cannabis strains that promote energy, creativity, and mental clarity, such as Super Lemon Haze, Blue Dream, Green Crack, Amnesia Haze, and Jack Herer, Sagittarius individuals can enhance their natural qualities and stay motivated and balanced in their daily lives. These strains offer a natural way to boost focus, reduce stress, and promote overall well-being, empowering Sagittarius to explore, learn, and grow with confidence and enthusiasm. Embracing the influence of Sagittarius can lead to a life filled with adventure, intellectual growth, and endless possibilities.

Check out my Virtual dispensary for all your hemp needs: https://shift.store/sg1fan23477/retail

Chapter 20: Capricorn: The Strategist

Traits of Capricorn

Capricorn, the tenth sign of the zodiac, is known as the strategist. Governed by Saturn, the planet of discipline, responsibility, and structure, Capricorn embodies the principles of ambition, practicality, and perseverance. As a cardinal earth sign, Capricorn is grounded, methodical, and highly goal-oriented. Understanding the core traits of Capricorn can help us appreciate their determined, disciplined, and strategic nature.

Key Traits of Capricorn:

1. **Ambitious and Goal-Oriented:** Capricorn individuals are highly ambitious and driven to achieve their goals. They have a clear vision of what they want to accomplish and are willing to put in the hard work to get there.

2. **Practical and Realistic:** Capricorn is known for their practicality and realistic approach to life. They focus on what is achievable and make decisions based on logic and reason.

3. **Disciplined and Responsible:** Capricorn possesses strong discipline and a sense of responsibility. They are reliable and take their commitments seriously, often taking on leadership roles and ensuring tasks are completed efficiently.

4. **Perseverance and Patience:** Capricorn has an incredible ability to persevere through challenges. They are patient and understand that success often requires time and sustained effort.

5. **Strategic and Methodical:** Capricorn is highly strategic and methodical in their approach. They plan carefully and think long-term, often devising detailed strategies to achieve their objectives.

6. **Reserved and Cautious:** Capricorn tends to be reserved and cautious, preferring to observe and analyze before taking action. They are not easily swayed by emotions and remain composed under pressure.
7. **Loyal and Dependable:** Capricorn is loyal and dependable, both in personal and professional relationships. They value trust and integrity and are committed to supporting those they care about.

Capricorn in Relationships:

- **Romantic Relationships:** In romantic relationships, Capricorn is devoted, loyal, and supportive. They seek partners who share their values and long-term goals. Their partners can expect a stable, committed relationship built on mutual respect and trust.
- **Friendships:** As friends, Capricorn is reliable, trustworthy, and supportive. They may not be the most outgoing, but they form deep, lasting friendships based on mutual respect and loyalty.
- **Family:** Within the family, Capricorn takes on a responsible and nurturing role. They value family traditions and work hard to create a secure and supportive environment. Their practical advice and guidance are often appreciated by family members.
- **Career:** In their careers, Capricorn excels in roles that require discipline, organization, and strategic thinking. They are often found in professions related to management, finance, engineering, and administration, where they can apply their skills and achieve long-term success.

Best Cannabis Strains for Capricorn

Given the disciplined and goal-oriented nature of Capricorn, the best cannabis strains for this sign should enhance their natural qualities and provide relaxation, mental clarity, and focus. Strains that promote relaxation, reduce stress, and enhance concentration can help Capricorn maintain their productivity and well-being.

OG Kush: Calming and Grounding

OG Kush is a hybrid strain known for its potent relaxing effects and ability to provide a sense of grounding. It is ideal for Capricorn individuals seeking to reduce stress and enhance focus.

- **Effects:** OG Kush offers a calming, euphoric high that helps to reduce stress and promote relaxation. Its grounding effects can enhance focus and provide a sense of stability, aligning well with Capricorn's disciplined and responsible nature.
- **Flavor and Aroma:** This strain has a complex aroma with notes of earth, pine, and citrus, contributing to its soothing and grounding properties.
- **Usage:** OG Kush is suitable for evening use or during times of high stress, helping Capricorn unwind and regain emotional balance.

Bubba Kush: Calming and Focused

Bubba Kush is an indica strain known for its strong calming effects and ability to promote relaxation. It is perfect for those seeking deep relaxation and mental clarity.

- **Effects:** Bubba Kush provides a heavy, calming high that promotes deep relaxation and stress relief. Its sedative effects help to reduce anxiety and enhance concentration, making it a perfect complement to Capricorn's need for comfort and stability.
- **Flavor and Aroma:** This strain has a sweet, earthy aroma with hints of coffee and chocolate, adding to its relaxing and grounding profile.
- **Usage:** Bubba Kush is best used in the evening or before bed to promote relaxation and focus, providing a sense of calm and clarity.

Northern Lights: Relaxing and Grounding

Northern Lights is a classic indica strain known for its deeply relaxing and calming effects. It is highly effective for those needing to unwind and achieve emotional tranquility.

- **Effects:** Northern Lights delivers a potent, body-focused high that promotes relaxation and sleep. Its calming effects help to alleviate stress, anxiety, and emotional tension, making it a perfect strain for grounding and focus.
- **Flavor and Aroma:** This strain has a sweet, earthy aroma with hints of pine and spice, adding to its comforting profile.
- **Usage:** Northern Lights is best used in the evening or before bed to help relax the body and mind, promoting restful sleep and emotional peace.

Granddaddy Purple: Relaxing and Comforting

Granddaddy Purple (GDP) is an indica strain known for its deeply relaxing and soothing effects. It is an excellent choice for Capricorn individuals who seek comfort and stress relief.

- **Effects:** Granddaddy Purple offers a calming, euphoric high that promotes relaxation and sleep. Its powerful effects help to reduce stress and anxiety, making it perfect for Capricorn's love of comfort and relaxation.
- **Flavor and Aroma:** This strain has a sweet, grape-like aroma with earthy undertones, contributing to its comforting and enjoyable experience.
- **Usage:** Granddaddy Purple is best used in the evening or before bed to help Capricorn unwind and achieve a deep, restful sleep.

Cannatonic: Relaxing and Uplifting

Cannatonic is a hybrid strain known for its balanced THC and CBD content, providing mild psychoactive effects and clear-headed relaxation.

- **Effects:** Cannatonic offers a relaxing, uplifting high that promotes mental clarity and focus. Its balanced THC and CBD content helps to reduce stress and enhance cognitive function without overwhelming euphoria.
- **Flavor and Aroma:** This strain has a mild, earthy aroma with hints of pine and citrus, contributing to its soothing effects.
- **Usage:** Cannatonic is suitable for daytime use, providing a balanced approach to relaxation and mental clarity, helping Capricorn stay productive and focused.

Conclusion

Capricorn, the strategist of the zodiac, is defined by their ambition, practicality, and disciplined approach to life. Understanding their core traits can help us appreciate their determined and strategic nature. By integrating specific cannabis strains that promote relaxation, mental clarity, and focus, such as OG Kush, Bubba Kush, Northern Lights, Granddaddy Purple, and Cannatonic, Capricorn individuals can enhance their natural qualities and maintain their productivity and well-being. These strains offer a natural way to boost focus, reduce stress, and promote overall well-being, empowering Capricorn to achieve their goals, build lasting success, and lead with confidence and integrity. Embracing the influence of Capricorn can lead to a life filled with strategic accomplishments, personal growth, and enduring achievements.

Check out my Virtual dispensary for all your hemp needs: https://shift.store/sg1fan23477/retail

Chapter 21: Aquarius: The Visionary

Traits of Aquarius

Aquarius, the eleventh sign of the zodiac, is known as the visionary. Governed by Uranus, the planet of innovation and change, and traditionally by Saturn, the planet of discipline and structure, Aquarius embodies the principles of originality, progressiveness, and humanitarianism. As a fixed air sign, Aquarius is intellectual, independent, and always looking toward the future. Understanding the core traits of Aquarius can help us appreciate their inventive, unconventional, and altruistic nature.

Key Traits of Aquarius:

1. **Innovative and Original:** Aquarius individuals are natural innovators. They are drawn to new ideas, technologies, and ways of thinking, always seeking to push the boundaries of what is possible.

2. **Intellectual and Analytical:** Aquarius possesses strong intellectual and analytical abilities. They enjoy exploring complex concepts and theories, often delving into scientific, technological, or philosophical pursuits.

3. **Independent and Free-Spirited:** Aquarius values their independence and freedom. They resist conformity and prefer to carve their own unique path in life.

4. **Humanitarian and Altruistic:** Aquarius is deeply concerned with social issues and the well-being of humanity. They are often involved in humanitarian efforts and advocate for progressive social change.

5. **Visionary and Forward-Thinking:** Aquarius is forward-thinking and visionary, always looking ahead to the future and considering the long-term implications of their actions.

6. **Unconventional and Eccentric:** Aquarius is known for their unconventional and sometimes eccentric nature. They are not afraid to stand out and embrace their individuality.

7. **Detached and Aloof:** Due to their intellectual focus, Aquarius can sometimes appear detached or aloof. They may struggle with expressing emotions and connecting on a deeply personal level.

Aquarius in Relationships:

- **Romantic Relationships:** In romantic relationships, Aquarius is loyal, intellectually stimulating, and adventurous. They seek partners who can appreciate their need for independence and share their passion for new ideas and experiences. Their partners can expect a relationship filled with intellectual engagement and mutual respect.

- **Friendships:** As friends, Aquarius is loyal, supportive, and engaging. They enjoy socializing and bringing people together, often organizing group activities and discussions. Their friends can rely on their innovative ideas and open-minded approach.

- **Family:** Within the family, Aquarius takes on a nurturing and supportive role. They value family bonds and work hard to create a loving and inclusive environment. Their intellectual curiosity often inspires family members to embrace new ideas and perspectives.

- **Career:** In their careers, Aquarius excels in roles that require creativity, innovation, and intellectual engagement. They are often found in professions related to science, technology, social work, and the arts, where they can use their visionary abilities to make a positive impact.

Best Cannabis Strains for Aquarius

Given the innovative and forward-thinking nature of Aquarius, the best cannabis strains for this sign should enhance their natural qualities and provide energy, creativity, and mental clarity. Strains that promote focus, creativity, and relaxation can help Aquarius stay motivated and balanced while exploring new ideas and experiences.

Sour Tangie: Uplifting and Energizing

Sour Tangie is a sativa-dominant hybrid known for its uplifting and energizing effects. It is perfect for Aquarius individuals seeking a boost in energy and creativity.

- **Effects:** Sour Tangie provides a strong, cerebral high that enhances focus, creativity, and motivation. Its energizing effects help combat fatigue and promote a sense of enthusiasm and optimism, aligning with Aquarius's growth-oriented nature.
- **Flavor and Aroma:** This strain has a tangy, citrusy aroma with sweet undertones, adding to its invigorating profile.
- **Usage:** Sour Tangie is ideal for daytime use, providing a sustained boost in energy and mental sharpness, helping Aquarius stay active and engaged.

Pineapple Express: Energizing and Creative

Pineapple Express is a hybrid strain known for its balanced effects, offering both mental stimulation and physical relaxation. It is a favorite for Aquarius individuals who seek a harmonious blend of energy and calmness.

- **Effects:** Pineapple Express provides a mild, euphoric high that promotes happiness and creativity. It enhances focus and productivity while also offering a subtle body relaxation, making it a versatile strain that resonates with Aquarius's vibrant and dynamic nature.

- **Flavor and Aroma:** This strain has a delightful tropical aroma with hints of pineapple and citrus, contributing to its refreshing and enjoyable effects.
- **Usage:** Pineapple Express is suitable for any time of day, particularly when a balanced approach to energy and relaxation is desired, helping Aquarius stay motivated and grounded.

Super Silver Haze: Creative and Energizing

Super Silver Haze is a sativa-dominant hybrid known for its uplifting and mood-enhancing effects. It is perfect for Aquarius individuals needing an emotional boost and mental clarity.

- **Effects:** Super Silver Haze delivers a cerebral, euphoric high that enhances mood and energy levels. It helps to reduce stress and anxiety while promoting a positive, optimistic outlook, aligning with Aquarius's innovative and forward-thinking qualities.
- **Flavor and Aroma:** This strain has a citrusy, earthy aroma with hints of sweetness, contributing to its energizing effects.
- **Usage:** Super Silver Haze is suitable for daytime use, providing a boost in energy and mood without causing sedation, helping Aquarius stay sharp and engaged.

Jack Herer: Creative and Euphoric

Named after the famous cannabis activist, Jack Herer is a well-balanced hybrid strain known for its potent, clear-headed effects and ability to enhance creativity and concentration.

- **Effects:** Jack Herer offers a blissful, euphoric high that stimulates both the mind and body. It promotes a sense of well-being and encourages creative thinking, making it a perfect complement to Aquarius's need for mental stimulation and social engagement.

- **Flavor and Aroma:** The strain has a distinctive aroma with notes of pine, earth, and citrus, contributing to its refreshing and energizing effects.
- **Usage:** Jack Herer is often used during creative endeavors or social activities, providing a burst of energy and inspiration without overwhelming the senses.

Amnesia Haze: Uplifting and Creative

Amnesia Haze is a sativa-dominant strain known for its uplifting and mood-enhancing effects. It is perfect for Aquarius individuals needing an emotional boost and mental clarity.

- **Effects:** Amnesia Haze delivers a cerebral, euphoric high that enhances mood and energy levels. It helps to reduce stress and anxiety while promoting a positive, optimistic outlook, aligning with Aquarius's dynamic and optimistic qualities.
- **Flavor and Aroma:** This strain has a citrusy, earthy aroma with hints of sweetness, contributing to its uplifting effects.
- **Usage:** Amnesia Haze is suitable for daytime use, providing a boost in energy and mood without causing sedation, helping Aquarius stay sharp and engaged.

Conclusion

Aquarius, the visionary of the zodiac, is defined by their innovative spirit, intellectual curiosity, and humanitarian values. Understanding their core traits can help us appreciate their dynamic and forward-thinking nature. By integrating specific cannabis strains that promote energy, creativity, and mental clarity, such as Sour Tangie, Pineapple Express, Super Silver Haze, Jack Herer, and Amnesia Haze, Aquarius individuals can enhance their natural qualities and stay motivated and balanced in their daily lives. These strains offer a natural way to boost focus, reduce stress, and promote overall well-being, empowering Aquarius to explore, innovate, and make a positive impact on the world with confidence and enthusiasm. Embracing the influence of Aquarius can lead to a life filled with visionary accomplishments, intellectual growth, and meaningful contributions to society.

Check out my Virtual dispensary for all your hemp needs: https://shift.store/sg1fan23477/retail

Chapter 22: Pisces: The Dreamer

Traits of Pisces

Pisces, the twelfth and final sign of the zodiac, is known as the dreamer. Governed by Neptune, the planet of intuition, dreams, and spirituality, Pisces embodies the principles of compassion, creativity, and sensitivity. As a mutable water sign, Pisces is adaptable, empathetic, and deeply connected to the emotional and spiritual realms. Understanding the core traits of Pisces can help us appreciate their imaginative, gentle, and mystical nature.

Key Traits of Pisces:

1. **Compassionate and Empathetic:** Pisces individuals are deeply compassionate and empathetic. They have a natural ability to understand and share the feelings of others, often putting themselves in others' shoes.

2. **Creative and Imaginative:** Pisces is highly creative and imaginative. They have a rich inner world and often express themselves through artistic pursuits such as music, writing, and visual arts.

3. **Intuitive and Spiritual:** Governed by Neptune, Pisces is highly intuitive and spiritually inclined. They are often drawn to mystical and esoteric subjects, seeking a deeper understanding of the universe.

4. **Adaptable and Flexible:** Pisces is adaptable and flexible, able to go with the flow and adjust to changing circumstances. They are not easily confined by rigid structures or routines.

5. **Gentle and Sensitive:** Pisces is gentle and sensitive, often feeling emotions intensely. They are kind-hearted and avoid conflict, seeking harmony and peace in their interactions.

6. **Selfless and Sacrificial:** Pisces is selfless and often willing to sacrifice their own needs for the sake of others. They derive fulfillment from helping and nurturing those around them.

7. **Dreamy and Idealistic:** Pisces tends to be dreamy and idealistic, sometimes struggling to distinguish between reality and fantasy. They often have a rosy view of the world and can be deeply idealistic.

Pisces in Relationships:

- **Romantic Relationships:** In romantic relationships, Pisces is affectionate, devoted, and deeply loving. They seek emotional and spiritual connection with their partners, often creating a nurturing and supportive bond. Their partners can expect a relationship filled with compassion, creativity, and deep emotional intimacy.

- **Friendships:** As friends, Pisces is loyal, supportive, and understanding. They are excellent listeners and provide a comforting presence. Their friends can rely on their empathy and willingness to offer emotional support.

- **Family:** Within the family, Pisces takes on a nurturing and compassionate role. They value family bonds and work hard to create a loving and harmonious environment. Their sensitivity and intuition help them connect deeply with family members.

- **Career:** In their careers, Pisces excels in roles that require creativity, empathy, and intuition. They are often found in professions related to the arts, healing, counseling, and spirituality, where they can use their talents to inspire and help others.

Best Cannabis Strains for Pisces

Given the compassionate and imaginative nature of Pisces, the best cannabis strains for this sign should enhance their natural qualities and provide relaxation, creativity, and emotional balance. Strains that promote relaxation, reduce stress, and enhance creativity can help Pisces maintain their emotional well-being and stay connected to their inner world.

Purple Kush: Deeply Relaxing and Soothing

Purple Kush is an indica strain known for its deeply relaxing and calming effects. It is highly effective for those seeking to unwind and achieve emotional tranquility.

- **Effects:** Purple Kush delivers a potent, body-focused high that promotes relaxation and sleep. Its calming effects help to alleviate stress, anxiety, and emotional tension, making it a perfect strain for grounding and focus.
- **Flavor and Aroma:** This strain has a sweet, earthy aroma with hints of grape and berry, contributing to its comforting profile.
- **Usage:** Purple Kush is best used in the evening or before bed to help relax the body and mind, promoting restful sleep and emotional peace.

Lavender: Tranquil and Soothing

Lavender is an indica-dominant strain known for its strong calming and sedative effects. It is ideal for those seeking deep relaxation and enhanced spiritual experiences.

- **Effects:** Lavender provides a heavy, tranquilizing high that eases the mind and body into a state of deep relaxation. Its calming effects help to quiet the mind and promote a sense of peace, making it perfect for meditation and emotional healing.
- **Flavor and Aroma:** This strain has a floral, lavender-like aroma with hints of herbs and spices, enhancing its soothing properties.

- **Usage:** Lavender is best used in the evening or during spiritual practices to promote relaxation, inner peace, and emotional balance.

Blue Dream: Relaxing and Uplifting

Blue Dream is a hybrid strain celebrated for its balanced effects that provide both relaxation and mental invigoration. It is an excellent choice for Pisces individuals who seek to enhance creativity and stress relief during transformational periods.

- **Effects:** Blue Dream offers a gentle, euphoric high that helps to calm the mind and uplift the spirit. It provides a sense of mental clarity and relaxation without sedation, making it ideal for creative projects and personal growth.
- **Flavor and Aroma:** This strain has a sweet, berry-like aroma with earthy undertones, contributing to its soothing effects.
- **Usage:** Blue Dream is suitable for any time of day, providing emotional stability and a positive mindset without overwhelming the senses, supporting deep transformation and healing.

Granddaddy Purple: Relaxing and Comforting

Granddaddy Purple (GDP) is an indica strain known for its deeply relaxing and soothing effects. It is an excellent choice for Pisces individuals who seek comfort and stress relief.

- **Effects:** Granddaddy Purple offers a calming, euphoric high that promotes relaxation and sleep. Its powerful effects help to reduce stress and anxiety, making it perfect for Pisces's love of comfort and relaxation.
- **Flavor and Aroma:** This strain has a sweet, grape-like aroma with earthy undertones, contributing to its comforting and enjoyable experience.

- **Usage:** Granddaddy Purple is best used in the evening or before bed to help Pisces unwind and achieve a deep, restful sleep.

Northern Lights: Relaxing and Grounding

Northern Lights is a classic indica strain known for its deeply relaxing and calming effects. It is highly effective for those needing to unwind and achieve emotional tranquility.

- **Effects:** Northern Lights delivers a potent, body-focused high that promotes relaxation and sleep. Its calming effects help to alleviate stress, anxiety, and emotional tension, making it a perfect strain for grounding and focus.
- **Flavor and Aroma:** This strain has a sweet, earthy aroma with hints of pine and spice, adding to its comforting profile.
- **Usage:** Northern Lights is best used in the evening or before bed to help relax the body and mind, promoting restful sleep and emotional peace.

Conclusion

Pisces, the dreamer of the zodiac, is defined by their compassion, creativity, and sensitivity. Understanding their core traits can help us appreciate their gentle and imaginative nature. By integrating specific cannabis strains that promote relaxation, creativity, and emotional balance, such as Purple Kush, Lavender, Blue Dream, Granddaddy Purple, and Northern Lights, Pisces individuals can enhance their natural qualities and maintain their emotional well-being. These strains offer a natural way to boost focus, reduce stress, and promote overall well-being, empowering Pisces to dream, create, and connect with their inner selves and the world around them. Embracing the influence of Pisces can lead to a life filled with compassion, creativity, and spiritual growth.

Check out my Virtual dispensary for all your hemp needs: https://shift.store/sg1fan23477/retail

Part III: Celestial Bodies and Their Influence

Chapter 23: The North Node: Destiny and Purpose
The Role of the North Node in Astrology

In astrology, the North Node represents our soul's path and purpose in this lifetime. It is a point in the sky where the Moon's orbit intersects the ecliptic, or the apparent path of the Sun. The North Node is directly opposite the South Node, which signifies our past life experiences and the qualities we have already mastered. While the South Node is about comfort zones and familiar patterns, the North Node challenges us to grow, evolve, and fulfill our highest potential.

Key Aspects of the North Node in Astrology:

1. **Life Purpose and Destiny:** The North Node symbolizes our life purpose and destiny. It points to the qualities we need to develop and the experiences we must embrace to achieve spiritual growth and fulfillment.

2. **Challenges and Growth:** The North Node represents areas of life that are initially uncomfortable and challenging but ultimately lead to significant personal growth and evolution.

3. **Balancing Karma:** The North Node, in conjunction with the South Node, highlights the balance between our past and future. While the South Node shows where we have been, the North Node shows where we are headed and what we need to learn.

4. **Individual Chart Significance:** The sign and house placement of the North Node in an individual's natal chart reveal specific themes and areas of life where growth and evolution are needed. Each person's North Node path is unique and deeply personal.

5. **Collective Influence:** The North Node also moves through the zodiac signs collectively, indicating themes of growth and development for society as a whole during its transit.

Interpreting the North Node in Different Signs:

- **Aries North Node:** Embrace independence, courage, and self-assertion. Focus on developing leadership skills and pursuing personal goals.
- **Taurus North Node:** Cultivate stability, security, and self-worth. Learn to appreciate the material world and build a solid foundation.
- **Gemini North Node:** Emphasize communication, learning, and adaptability. Seek to share knowledge and engage in meaningful conversations.
- **Cancer North Node:** Nurture emotional sensitivity, family bonds, and home life. Develop a sense of belonging and care for others.
- **Leo North Node:** Foster creativity, self-expression, and confidence. Shine your light and inspire others with your unique talents.
- **Virgo North Node:** Focus on practicality, service, and attention to detail. Strive for order, health, and a disciplined approach to life.
- **Libra North Node:** Develop harmony, relationships, and diplomacy. Seek balance and fairness in interactions with others.
- **Scorpio North Node:** Embrace transformation, intensity, and deep emotional connections. Learn to release control and trust the process of change.
- **Sagittarius North Node:** Pursue adventure, higher learning, and spiritual growth. Expand your horizons and seek truth and wisdom.

- **Capricorn North Node:** Cultivate ambition, discipline, and responsibility. Focus on long-term goals and professional achievements.
- **Aquarius North Node:** Foster innovation, individuality, and humanitarianism. Contribute to the greater good and embrace progressive ideas.
- **Pisces North Node:** Nurture compassion, intuition, and spiritual connection. Learn to go with the flow and trust your inner guidance.

Cannabis Strains for Aligning with Destiny

To align with the transformative and growth-oriented nature of the North Node, certain cannabis strains can help enhance focus, motivation, and mental clarity. These strains support personal development, encouraging individuals to embrace their life's purpose and navigate the challenges along the way.

Durban Poison: Energizing and Focused

Durban Poison is a pure sativa strain known for its invigorating and uplifting effects. It is ideal for those seeking to enhance focus, motivation, and mental clarity.

- **Effects:** Durban Poison delivers a powerful, cerebral high that promotes energy, focus, and creativity. Its stimulating effects help to combat fatigue and encourage productive activities, aligning with the North Node's call for growth and evolution.
- **Flavor and Aroma:** This strain has a sweet, earthy aroma with hints of pine and citrus, contributing to its refreshing and invigorating profile.
- **Usage:** Durban Poison is suitable for daytime use, providing a sustained boost in energy and mental sharpness, helping individuals stay active and engaged in their personal development.

Green Crack: Energizing and Motivating

Green Crack, despite its controversial name, is a pure sativa strain famed for its sharp, invigorating effects. It is perfect for those needing a substantial energy boost and mental clarity to align with their destiny.

- **Effects:** Green Crack delivers a potent cerebral high that enhances focus, energy, and motivation. Its effects are long-lasting and can help combat stress and fatigue, making it an excellent complement to the North Node's call for growth and transformation.
- **Flavor and Aroma:** This strain has a tangy, fruity flavor reminiscent of mango, with an earthy undertone that adds to its vibrant profile.
- **Usage:** Green Crack is best used during the day when mental alertness and physical activity are required, helping individuals tackle tasks with enthusiasm and vigor.

Super Silver Haze: Creative and Energizing

Super Silver Haze is a sativa-dominant hybrid known for its uplifting and mood-enhancing effects. It is perfect for those seeking an emotional boost and mental clarity.

- **Effects:** Super Silver Haze delivers a cerebral, euphoric high that enhances mood and energy levels. It helps to reduce stress and anxiety while promoting a positive, optimistic outlook, aligning with the North Node's transformative and forward-thinking qualities.
- **Flavor and Aroma:** This strain has a citrusy, earthy aroma with hints of sweetness, contributing to its energizing effects.
- **Usage:** Super Silver Haze is suitable for daytime use, providing a boost in energy and mood without causing sedation, helping individuals stay sharp and engaged.

Jack Herer: Creative and Euphoric

Named after the famous cannabis activist, Jack Herer is a well-balanced hybrid strain known for its potent, clear-headed effects and ability to enhance creativity and concentration.

- **Effects:** Jack Herer offers a blissful, euphoric high that stimulates both the mind and body. It promotes a sense of well-being and encourages creative thinking, making it a perfect complement to the North Node's call for personal growth and self-discovery.
- **Flavor and Aroma:** The strain has a distinctive aroma with notes of pine, earth, and citrus, contributing to its refreshing and energizing effects.
- **Usage:** Jack Herer is often used during creative endeavors or personal development activities, providing a burst of energy and inspiration without overwhelming the senses.

Amnesia Haze: Uplifting and Creative

Amnesia Haze is a sativa-dominant strain known for its uplifting and mood-enhancing effects. It is ideal for those needing an emotional boost and mental clarity to align with their life's purpose.

- **Effects:** Amnesia Haze delivers a cerebral, euphoric high that enhances mood and energy levels. It helps to reduce stress and anxiety while promoting a positive, optimistic outlook, aligning with the North Node's dynamic and transformative qualities.
- **Flavor and Aroma:** This strain has a citrusy, earthy aroma with hints of sweetness, contributing to its uplifting effects.
- **Usage:** Amnesia Haze is suitable for daytime use, providing a boost in energy and mood without causing sedation, helping individuals stay sharp and engaged in their personal growth journey.

Conclusion

The North Node in astrology represents our soul's path and purpose, guiding us toward growth, transformation, and fulfillment. Understanding its influence can help us embrace our life's challenges and opportunities with clarity and determination. By integrating specific cannabis strains that promote energy, creativity, and mental clarity, such as Durban Poison, Green Crack, Super Silver Haze, Jack Herer, and Amnesia Haze, individuals can enhance their natural qualities and stay motivated and balanced while aligning with their destiny. These strains offer a natural way to boost focus, reduce stress, and promote overall well-being, empowering individuals to pursue their highest potential and fulfill their life's purpose. Embracing the influence of the North Node can lead to a life filled with meaningful growth, personal transformation, and spiritual fulfillment.

Check out my Virtual dispensary for all your hemp needs: https://shift.store/sg1fan23477/retail

Chapter 24: The South Node: Karmic Lessons
The Role of the South Node in Astrology

In astrology, the South Node represents our past lives, karmic lessons, and the innate qualities and habits we bring into this lifetime. It is the point directly opposite the North Node on the astrological chart. While the North Node symbolizes our future growth and the qualities we need to develop, the South Node highlights our comfort zones and the areas where we may rely too heavily on past patterns. Understanding the South Node can help us recognize the habits we need to release and the lessons we need to learn to evolve and fulfill our potential.

Key Aspects of the South Node in Astrology:

1. **Past Life Experiences:** The South Node is associated with past life experiences and the qualities we have already mastered. It represents the skills and attributes that come naturally to us.

2. **Comfort Zones:** The South Node indicates our comfort zones, where we feel safe and secure. While these areas are familiar and easy, they can also hold us back from growth and new experiences.

3. **Karmic Lessons:** The South Node highlights the karmic lessons we need to learn in this lifetime. It shows the behaviors and patterns we need to overcome to move forward on our soul's journey.

4. **Balance with the North Node:** The South Node and North Node work together to create balance. While the North Node points to our future path, the South Node reminds us of our past and the importance of integrating past lessons with new growth.

5. **Individual Chart Significance:** The sign and house placement of the South Node in an individual's natal chart reveal specific

themes and areas of life where past patterns and karmic lessons are most influential.

Interpreting the South Node in Different Signs:

- **Aries South Node:** Indicates a past focus on independence and self-assertion. The lesson is to balance personal initiative with cooperation and partnership (North Node in Libra).
- **Taurus South Node:** Indicates a past focus on material security and stability. The lesson is to balance comfort with emotional depth and transformation (North Node in Scorpio).
- **Gemini South Node:** Indicates a past focus on communication and intellectual pursuits. The lesson is to balance curiosity with philosophical understanding and broader vision (North Node in Sagittarius).
- **Cancer South Node:** Indicates a past focus on home and family. The lesson is to balance nurturing with ambition and public life (North Node in Capricorn).
- **Leo South Node:** Indicates a past focus on self-expression and recognition. The lesson is to balance personal creativity with group dynamics and humanitarian efforts (North Node in Aquarius).
- **Virgo South Node:** Indicates a past focus on practicality and service. The lesson is to balance detail-oriented work with spiritual awareness and compassion (North Node in Pisces).
- **Libra South Node:** Indicates a past focus on relationships and harmony. The lesson is to balance cooperation with self-assertion and independence (North Node in Aries).
- **Scorpio South Node:** Indicates a past focus on intensity and transformation. The lesson is to balance emotional depth with stability and material security (North Node in Taurus).

- **Sagittarius South Node:** Indicates a past focus on adventure and higher learning. The lesson is to balance exploration with communication and daily interactions (North Node in Gemini).
- **Capricorn South Node:** Indicates a past focus on ambition and responsibility. The lesson is to balance career with home and family life (North Node in Cancer).
- **Aquarius South Node:** Indicates a past focus on innovation and individuality. The lesson is to balance progressiveness with personal creativity and self-expression (North Node in Leo).
- **Pisces South Node:** Indicates a past focus on spirituality and compassion. The lesson is to balance spiritual awareness with practical service and organization (North Node in Virgo).

Cannabis Strains for Understanding Past Lessons

To understand and integrate the karmic lessons represented by the South Node, certain cannabis strains can help enhance relaxation, introspection, and emotional balance. These strains support self-reflection, encouraging individuals to release past patterns and embrace new growth.

Granddaddy Purple: Relaxing and Comforting

Granddaddy Purple (GDP) is an indica strain known for its deeply relaxing and soothing effects. It is highly effective for those seeking comfort and stress relief while reflecting on past experiences.

- **Effects:** Granddaddy Purple offers a calming, euphoric high that promotes relaxation and sleep. Its powerful effects help to reduce stress and anxiety, making it perfect for introspection and emotional healing.
- **Flavor and Aroma:** This strain has a sweet, grape-like aroma with earthy undertones, contributing to its comforting and enjoyable experience.

- **Usage:** Granddaddy Purple is best used in the evening or before bed to help individuals unwind and achieve a deep, restful sleep, facilitating reflective and meditative states.

Northern Lights: Relaxing and Grounding

Northern Lights is a classic indica strain known for its deeply relaxing and calming effects. It is highly effective for those needing to unwind and achieve emotional tranquility.

- **Effects:** Northern Lights delivers a potent, body-focused high that promotes relaxation and sleep. Its calming effects help to alleviate stress, anxiety, and emotional tension, making it a perfect strain for grounding and focus.
- **Flavor and Aroma:** This strain has a sweet, earthy aroma with hints of pine and spice, adding to its comforting profile.
- **Usage:** Northern Lights is best used in the evening or before bed to help relax the body and mind, promoting restful sleep and emotional peace, aiding in the reflection of past lessons.

Blueberry: Relaxing and Uplifting

Blueberry is an indica-dominant strain known for its relaxing and euphoric effects. It is perfect for those seeking a sense of well-being and introspection.

- **Effects:** Blueberry offers a calming, euphoric high that promotes relaxation and happiness. Its soothing effects can enhance feelings of contentment and introspection, making it ideal for reflecting on past experiences and lessons.
- **Flavor and Aroma:** This strain has a sweet, berry-like aroma with earthy undertones, adding to its delightful sensory experience.
- **Usage:** Blueberry is suitable for any time of day, providing relaxation and a positive mood that enhances reflective and meditative states.

Bubba Kush: Calming and Grounded

Bubba Kush is an indica strain known for its strong calming effects and ability to promote relaxation. It is perfect for those seeking deep relaxation and mental clarity.

- **Effects:** Bubba Kush provides a heavy, calming high that promotes deep relaxation and stress relief. Its sedative effects help to reduce anxiety and enhance concentration, making it a perfect complement to introspective and reflective activities.
- **Flavor and Aroma:** This strain has a sweet, earthy aroma with hints of coffee and chocolate, adding to its relaxing and grounding profile.
- **Usage:** Bubba Kush is best used in the evening or before bed to promote relaxation and focus, providing a sense of calm and clarity for reflecting on past lessons.

Lavender: Tranquil and Soothing

Lavender is an indica-dominant strain known for its strong calming and sedative effects. It is ideal for those seeking deep relaxation and enhanced spiritual experiences.

- **Effects:** Lavender provides a heavy, tranquilizing high that eases the mind and body into a state of deep relaxation. Its calming effects help to quiet the mind and promote a sense of peace, making it perfect for meditation and emotional healing.
- **Flavor and Aroma:** This strain has a floral, lavender-like aroma with hints of herbs and spices, enhancing its soothing properties.
- **Usage:** Lavender is best used in the evening or during spiritual practices to promote relaxation, inner peace, and emotional balance, supporting reflection on past karmic lessons.

Conclusion

The South Node in astrology represents our past lives, karmic lessons, and the qualities we have already mastered. Understanding its influence can help us recognize the habits we need to release and the lessons we need to learn to evolve and fulfill our potential. By integrating specific cannabis strains that promote relaxation, introspection, and emotional balance, such as Granddaddy Purple, Northern Lights, Blueberry, Bubba Kush, and Lavender, individuals can enhance their natural qualities and maintain their emotional well-being while reflecting on past experiences. These strains offer a natural way to boost focus, reduce stress, and promote overall well-being, empowering individuals to understand and integrate their karmic lessons and embrace new growth. Embracing the influence of the South Node can lead to a life filled with meaningful growth, personal transformation, and spiritual fulfillment.

Check out my Virtual dispensary for all your hemp needs: https://shift.store/sg1fan23477/retail

Chapter 25: Chiron: The Wounded Healer
The Influence of Chiron

In astrology, Chiron is known as the "Wounded Healer." It represents our deepest wounds and the healing journey we undertake to overcome them. Named after the centaur Chiron from Greek mythology, who was a wise teacher and healer despite his own incurable wound, Chiron's placement in our natal chart highlights areas where we have been hurt and where we have the potential to become sources of profound wisdom and healing for ourselves and others.

Key Aspects of Chiron in Astrology:

1. **Deep Wounds:** Chiron represents the core wounds we carry, often from early life experiences or past lives. These wounds can be physical, emotional, psychological, or spiritual.

2. **Healing Journey:** The presence of Chiron in our chart signifies the healing journey we must undertake. This journey is about acknowledging our pain, understanding its origins, and finding ways to heal and grow beyond it.

3. **Empathy and Compassion:** Through our own experiences of suffering, Chiron bestows upon us the gift of empathy and compassion. We become more attuned to the pain of others and are often driven to help them heal.

4. **Wisdom and Teaching:** Chiron also represents the wisdom and teaching that come from our healing process. As we heal ourselves, we gain insights and knowledge that we can share with others, often becoming teachers or healers in our own right.

5. **Integration with the Natal Chart:** Chiron's influence is deeply personal and varies based on its sign and house placement in an

individual's natal chart. This placement reveals the specific nature of our wounds and the path to healing.

Interpreting Chiron in Different Signs:

- **Aries Chiron:** Wounds related to self-identity and assertion. Healing involves embracing self-worth and developing confidence.
- **Taurus Chiron:** Wounds related to security and self-worth. Healing involves finding inner stability and valuing oneself beyond material possessions.
- **Gemini Chiron:** Wounds related to communication and self-expression. Healing involves embracing one's voice and communicating authentically.
- **Cancer Chiron:** Wounds related to family and emotional security. Healing involves nurturing oneself and creating a sense of home within.
- **Leo Chiron:** Wounds related to self-expression and recognition. Healing involves embracing one's creativity and finding joy in self-expression.
- **Virgo Chiron:** Wounds related to perfectionism and service. Healing involves accepting imperfections and finding balance in serving others and oneself.
- **Libra Chiron:** Wounds related to relationships and balance. Healing involves developing healthy relationships and finding inner harmony.
- **Scorpio Chiron:** Wounds related to power and transformation. Healing involves embracing one's inner power and navigating deep emotional changes.
- **Sagittarius Chiron:** Wounds related to belief systems and freedom. Healing involves finding personal truth and embracing one's spiritual journey.

- **Capricorn Chiron:** Wounds related to achievement and responsibility. Healing involves finding self-worth beyond societal expectations and embracing personal goals.
- **Aquarius Chiron:** Wounds related to individuality and belonging. Healing involves embracing one's uniqueness and finding community.
- **Pisces Chiron:** Wounds related to spirituality and boundaries. Healing involves developing healthy boundaries and embracing spiritual connections.

Cannabis Strains for Healing and Introspection

To support the healing and introspective journey represented by Chiron, certain cannabis strains can help enhance relaxation, mental clarity, and emotional balance. These strains support self-reflection, encouraging individuals to address their wounds and embark on their healing path.

Blue Dream: Creative and Uplifting

Blue Dream is a hybrid strain celebrated for its balanced effects that provide both relaxation and mental invigoration. It is an excellent choice for individuals seeking to enhance creativity and introspection during their healing journey.

- **Effects:** Blue Dream offers a gentle, euphoric high that helps to calm the mind and uplift the spirit. It provides a sense of mental clarity and relaxation without sedation, making it ideal for creative projects and personal reflection.
- **Flavor and Aroma:** This strain has a sweet, berry-like aroma with earthy undertones, contributing to its soothing effects.
- **Usage:** Blue Dream is suitable for any time of day, providing emotional stability and a positive mindset without overwhelming the senses, supporting deep introspection and healing.

OG Kush: Calming and Grounding

OG Kush is a hybrid strain known for its potent relaxing effects and ability to provide a sense of grounding. It is ideal for those seeking to reduce stress and enhance focus during their healing journey.

- **Effects:** OG Kush offers a calming, euphoric high that helps to reduce stress and promote relaxation. Its grounding effects can enhance focus and provide a sense of stability, aligning well with the need for emotional healing and introspection.
- **Flavor and Aroma:** This strain has a complex aroma with notes of earth, pine, and citrus, contributing to its soothing and grounding properties.
- **Usage:** OG Kush is suitable for evening use or during times of high stress, helping individuals unwind and regain emotional balance, facilitating reflective and meditative states.

Lavender: Tranquil and Soothing

Lavender is an indica-dominant strain known for its strong calming and sedative effects. It is ideal for those seeking deep relaxation and enhanced spiritual experiences during their healing journey.

- **Effects:** Lavender provides a heavy, tranquilizing high that eases the mind and body into a state of deep relaxation. Its calming effects help to quiet the mind and promote a sense of peace, making it perfect for meditation and emotional healing.
- **Flavor and Aroma:** This strain has a floral, lavender-like aroma with hints of herbs and spices, enhancing its soothing properties.
- **Usage:** Lavender is best used in the evening or during spiritual practices to promote relaxation, inner peace, and emotional balance, supporting reflection on past wounds and healing.

Northern Lights: Relaxing and Grounding

Northern Lights is a classic indica strain known for its deeply relaxing and calming effects. It is highly effective for those needing to unwind and achieve emotional tranquility during their healing journey.

- **Effects:** Northern Lights delivers a potent, body-focused high that promotes relaxation and sleep. Its calming effects help to alleviate stress, anxiety, and emotional tension, making it a perfect strain for grounding and focus.
- **Flavor and Aroma:** This strain has a sweet, earthy aroma with hints of pine and spice, adding to its comforting profile.
- **Usage:** Northern Lights is best used in the evening or before bed to help relax the body and mind, promoting restful sleep and emotional peace, aiding in the reflection of past wounds and healing.

Harlequin: Clear-Headed and Focused

Harlequin is a sativa-dominant strain known for its high CBD content and clear-headed effects. It is an excellent choice for individuals who seek mental clarity and focus without intense psychoactive effects during their healing journey.

- **Effects:** Harlequin offers a balanced, clear-headed high that enhances focus and concentration. Its high CBD content helps to reduce anxiety and promote mental calmness, making it ideal for introspection and personal growth.
- **Flavor and Aroma:** This strain has an earthy, woody aroma with hints of mango and citrus, contributing to its refreshing profile.
- **Usage:** Harlequin is suitable for daytime use, providing mental clarity and focus without overwhelming psychoactive effects, helping individuals stay sharp and engaged in their healing journey.

Conclusion

Chiron, the wounded healer in astrology, represents our deepest wounds and the journey of healing and transformation. Understanding its influence can help us embrace our pain, learn from it, and become sources of healing for ourselves and others. By integrating specific cannabis strains that promote relaxation, mental clarity, and emotional balance, such as Blue Dream, OG Kush, Lavender, Northern Lights, and Harlequin, individuals can enhance their natural qualities and maintain their emotional well-being while reflecting on past wounds. These strains offer a natural way to boost focus, reduce stress, and promote overall well-being, empowering individuals to understand and heal their deepest wounds and embrace their path to wholeness. Embracing the influence of Chiron can lead to a life filled with meaningful growth, personal transformation, and profound healing.

Check out my Virtual dispensary for all your hemp needs: https://shift.store/sg1fan23477/retail

Chapter 26: Ceres: Nurturing and Growth

The Impact of Ceres

In astrology, Ceres is a dwarf planet that symbolizes nurturing, growth, and the cycles of nature. Named after the Roman goddess of agriculture and fertility, Ceres represents the nurturing aspects of life, our relationship with food and the Earth, and how we care for ourselves and others. Ceres' placement in our natal chart highlights how we give and receive nurturing, our attitudes toward self-care, and our capacity for growth and transformation through nurturing activities.

Key Aspects of Ceres in Astrology:

1. **Nurturing and Care:** Ceres represents how we nurture and care for others and ourselves. It influences our ability to provide support, comfort, and nourishment to those around us.
2. **Growth and Abundance:** As the goddess of agriculture, Ceres symbolizes growth and abundance. It highlights our relationship with the Earth, food, and the cycles of nature that sustain life.
3. **Parenting and Maternal Instincts:** Ceres is closely associated with maternal instincts and parenting. It reflects our approach to caregiving and the nurturing we received in childhood.
4. **Loss and Grief:** Ceres also encompasses themes of loss and grief, as the mythological Ceres experienced the loss of her daughter, Persephone. It represents the cycles of life, death, and rebirth.

5. **Self-Care and Health:** Ceres influences our attitudes toward self-care, health, and wellness. It highlights the importance of nurturing our bodies and minds through healthy habits and routines.

Interpreting Ceres in Different Signs:

- **Aries Ceres:** Nurtures through action and independence. Growth comes from encouraging self-reliance and assertiveness.
- **Taurus Ceres:** Nurtures through stability and sensory pleasures. Growth comes from creating a secure and comfortable environment.
- **Gemini Ceres:** Nurtures through communication and intellectual stimulation. Growth comes from encouraging curiosity and learning.
- **Cancer Ceres:** Nurtures through emotional support and care. Growth comes from fostering a sense of belonging and security.
- **Leo Ceres:** Nurtures through creativity and recognition. Growth comes from encouraging self-expression and confidence.
- **Virgo Ceres:** Nurtures through practical support and service. Growth comes from promoting health, organization, and efficiency.
- **Libra Ceres:** Nurtures through balance and harmony. Growth comes from fostering relationships and creating a peaceful environment.
- **Scorpio Ceres:** Nurtures through transformation and deep emotional connections. Growth comes from embracing change and fostering intimacy.
- **Sagittarius Ceres:** Nurtures through adventure and exploration. Growth comes from encouraging freedom, learning, and spiritual growth.
- **Capricorn Ceres:** Nurtures through discipline and structure. Growth comes from promoting responsibility and long-term planning.

- **Aquarius Ceres:** Nurtures through innovation and community. Growth comes from encouraging individuality and social progress.
- **Pisces Ceres:** Nurtures through compassion and empathy. Growth comes from fostering spiritual connection and emotional healing.

Cannabis Strains for Nurturing and Growth

To support the nurturing and growth-oriented influence of Ceres, certain cannabis strains can help enhance relaxation, mental clarity, and emotional balance. These strains support self-care, encouraging individuals to nurture themselves and others, promoting overall well-being and growth.

Harlequin: Clear-Headed and Focused

Harlequin is a sativa-dominant strain known for its high CBD content and clear-headed effects. It is an excellent choice for individuals seeking mental clarity and focus without intense psychoactive effects during their nurturing activities.

- **Effects:** Harlequin offers a balanced, clear-headed high that enhances focus and concentration. Its high CBD content helps to reduce anxiety and promote mental calmness, making it ideal for nurturing and self-care activities.
- **Flavor and Aroma:** This strain has an earthy, woody aroma with hints of mango and citrus, contributing to its refreshing profile.
- **Usage:** Harlequin is suitable for daytime use, providing mental clarity and focus without overwhelming psychoactive effects, helping individuals stay sharp and engaged in their nurturing activities.

ACDC: Clear-Headed and Relaxing

ACDC is a hybrid strain renowned for its high CBD content and minimal psychoactive effects. It is perfect for individuals seeking relaxation and mental clarity without the high.

- **Effects:** ACDC provides a relaxing, clear-headed high that enhances focus and reduces stress. Its high CBD content helps to calm the mind and body, making it suitable for tasks requiring mental clarity and composure.
- **Flavor and Aroma:** This strain has a sweet, earthy aroma with hints of citrus and pine, adding to its calming effects.
- **Usage:** ACDC is best used during the day when mental alertness and relaxation are needed, providing a clear mind and calm demeanor for nurturing and growth activities.

Lavender: Tranquil and Soothing

Lavender is an indica-dominant strain known for its strong calming and sedative effects. It is ideal for those seeking deep relaxation and enhanced spiritual experiences during their nurturing journey.

- **Effects:** Lavender provides a heavy, tranquilizing high that eases the mind and body into a state of deep relaxation. Its calming effects help to quiet the mind and promote a sense of peace, making it perfect for meditation and emotional healing.
- **Flavor and Aroma:** This strain has a floral, lavender-like aroma with hints of herbs and spices, enhancing its soothing properties.
- **Usage:** Lavender is best used in the evening or during spiritual practices to promote relaxation, inner peace, and emotional balance, supporting nurturing and self-care activities.

Northern Lights: Relaxing and Grounding

Northern Lights is a classic indica strain known for its deeply relaxing and calming effects. It is highly effective for those needing to unwind and achieve emotional tranquility during their nurturing journey.

- **Effects:** Northern Lights delivers a potent, body-focused high that promotes relaxation and sleep. Its calming effects help to alleviate stress, anxiety, and emotional tension, making it a perfect strain for grounding and focus.
- **Flavor and Aroma:** This strain has a sweet, earthy aroma with hints of pine and spice, adding to its comforting profile.
- **Usage:** Northern Lights is best used in the evening or before bed to help relax the body and mind, promoting restful sleep and emotional peace, aiding in nurturing and growth activities.

Blue Dream: Creative and Uplifting

Blue Dream is a hybrid strain celebrated for its balanced effects that provide both relaxation and mental invigoration. It is an excellent choice for individuals seeking to enhance creativity and stress relief during their nurturing journey.

- **Effects:** Blue Dream offers a gentle, euphoric high that helps to calm the mind and uplift the spirit. It provides a sense of mental clarity and relaxation without sedation, making it ideal for creative projects and personal growth.
- **Flavor and Aroma:** This strain has a sweet, berry-like aroma with earthy undertones, contributing to its soothing effects.
- **Usage:** Blue Dream is suitable for any time of day, providing emotional stability and a positive mindset without overwhelming the senses, supporting nurturing and self-care activities.

Conclusion

Ceres, the nurturing and growth-oriented influence in astrology, represents our capacity to nurture ourselves and others, fostering growth and transformation. Understanding its impact can help us embrace our nurturing nature, develop healthy self-care habits, and support the well-being of those around us. By integrating specific cannabis strains that promote relaxation, mental clarity, and emotional balance, such as Harlequin, ACDC, Lavender, Northern Lights, and Blue Dream, individuals can enhance their natural qualities and maintain their emotional well-being while engaging in nurturing activities. These strains offer a natural way to boost focus, reduce stress, and promote overall well-being, empowering individuals to nurture themselves and others, fostering growth and transformation. Embracing the influence of Ceres can lead to a life filled with nurturing care, personal growth, and abundant well-being.

Check out my Virtual dispensary for all your hemp needs: https://shift.store/sg1fan23477/retail

Chapter 27: Pallas: Wisdom and Creativity
The Role of Pallas

In astrology, Pallas (also known as Pallas Athena) is an asteroid that symbolizes wisdom, creativity, strategy, and intellect. Named after the Greek goddess of wisdom and war, Pallas represents our capacity for strategic thinking, creative problem-solving, and the ability to blend intellect with intuition. Pallas' placement in our natal chart highlights how we approach challenges, our creative expression, and our innate wisdom.

Key Aspects of Pallas in Astrology:

1. **Strategic Thinking:** Pallas represents our ability to think strategically and approach problems with a clear, analytical mind. It influences how we develop plans and strategies to achieve our goals.
2. **Creative Expression:** Pallas is associated with creativity and artistic expression. It highlights our talents in the arts and our ability to create beauty through various forms of expression.
3. **Intellect and Wisdom:** Pallas embodies intellectual prowess and wisdom. It reflects our ability to learn, understand complex concepts, and apply knowledge in practical ways.
4. **Integration of Intuition and Logic:** Pallas symbolizes the integration of intuition and logic. It represents our capacity to blend rational thinking with intuitive insights to make well-rounded decisions.

5. **Healing and Mediation:** Pallas is also connected to healing and mediation. It reflects our ability to find balanced solutions and bring harmony to conflicting situations.

Interpreting Pallas in Different Signs:

- **Aries Pallas:** Strategic thinking and creativity are expressed through action and innovation. Wisdom comes from embracing new challenges and pioneering ideas.
- **Taurus Pallas:** Strategic thinking and creativity are grounded in practicality and sensory experiences. Wisdom comes from creating beauty and stability through tangible means.
- **Gemini Pallas:** Strategic thinking and creativity are expressed through communication and intellectual pursuits. Wisdom comes from exploring diverse ideas and sharing knowledge.
- **Cancer Pallas:** Strategic thinking and creativity are nurtured through emotional intelligence and care. Wisdom comes from understanding and supporting others' needs.
- **Leo Pallas:** Strategic thinking and creativity are expressed through self-expression and leadership. Wisdom comes from inspiring and guiding others with confidence.
- **Virgo Pallas:** Strategic thinking and creativity are grounded in precision and service. Wisdom comes from practical problem-solving and attention to detail.
- **Libra Pallas:** Strategic thinking and creativity are expressed through harmony and balance. Wisdom comes from fostering relationships and creating aesthetic beauty.
- **Scorpio Pallas:** Strategic thinking and creativity are rooted in transformation and depth. Wisdom comes from embracing change and uncovering hidden truths.
- **Sagittarius Pallas:** Strategic thinking and creativity are expressed through exploration and philosophy. Wisdom comes from seeking knowledge and expanding horizons.

- **Capricorn Pallas:** Strategic thinking and creativity are grounded in discipline and structure. Wisdom comes from achieving long-term goals and building lasting success.
- **Aquarius Pallas:** Strategic thinking and creativity are expressed through innovation and community. Wisdom comes from embracing individuality and promoting progressive change.
- **Pisces Pallas:** Strategic thinking and creativity are nurtured through spirituality and compassion. Wisdom comes from connecting with the divine and fostering empathy.

Cannabis Strains for Wisdom and Creativity

To support the wisdom and creativity represented by Pallas, certain cannabis strains can help enhance mental clarity, focus, and inspiration. These strains support creative expression and strategic thinking, encouraging individuals to tap into their innate wisdom and problem-solving abilities.

Pineapple Express: Energizing and Creative

Pineapple Express is a hybrid strain known for its balanced effects, offering both mental stimulation and physical relaxation. It is a favorite for individuals seeking a harmonious blend of energy and calmness to enhance creativity and wisdom.

- **Effects:** Pineapple Express provides a mild, euphoric high that promotes happiness and creativity. It enhances focus and productivity while also offering a subtle body relaxation, making it a versatile strain that resonates with strategic thinking and creative problem-solving.
- **Flavor and Aroma:** This strain has a delightful tropical aroma with hints of pineapple and citrus, contributing to its refreshing and enjoyable effects.
- **Usage:** Pineapple Express is suitable for any time of day, particularly when a balanced approach to energy and relaxation is

desired, helping individuals stay motivated and grounded while engaging in creative and strategic activities.

Sour Tangie: Uplifting and Energizing

Sour Tangie is a sativa-dominant hybrid known for its uplifting and energizing effects. It is perfect for individuals seeking a boost in energy and creativity to enhance their strategic thinking and problem-solving abilities.

- **Effects:** Sour Tangie provides a strong, cerebral high that enhances focus, creativity, and motivation. Its energizing effects help combat fatigue and promote a sense of enthusiasm and optimism, aligning with the need for innovative thinking and creative expression.
- **Flavor and Aroma:** This strain has a tangy, citrusy aroma with sweet undertones, adding to its invigorating profile.
- **Usage:** Sour Tangie is ideal for daytime use, providing a sustained boost in energy and mental sharpness, helping individuals stay active and engaged in their creative and strategic pursuits.

Super Lemon Haze: Creative and Energizing

Super Lemon Haze is a sativa-dominant hybrid known for its uplifting and mood-enhancing effects. It is perfect for individuals needing an emotional boost and mental clarity to enhance their strategic thinking and creative problem-solving abilities.

- **Effects:** Super Lemon Haze delivers a cerebral, euphoric high that enhances mood and energy levels. It helps to reduce stress and anxiety while promoting a positive, optimistic outlook, aligning with the dynamic and innovative qualities of Pallas.
- **Flavor and Aroma:** This strain has a citrusy, earthy aroma with hints of sweetness, contributing to its energizing effects.

- **Usage:** Super Lemon Haze is suitable for daytime use, providing a boost in energy and mood without causing sedation, helping individuals stay sharp and engaged in their creative and strategic pursuits.

Jack Herer: Creative and Euphoric

Named after the famous cannabis activist, Jack Herer is a well-balanced hybrid strain known for its potent, clear-headed effects and ability to enhance creativity and concentration.

- **Effects:** Jack Herer offers a blissful, euphoric high that stimulates both the mind and body. It promotes a sense of well-being and encourages creative thinking, making it a perfect complement to the need for mental stimulation and strategic problem-solving.
- **Flavor and Aroma:** The strain has a distinctive aroma with notes of pine, earth, and citrus, contributing to its refreshing and energizing effects.
- **Usage:** Jack Herer is often used during creative endeavors or strategic planning activities, providing a burst of energy and inspiration without overwhelming the senses.

Amnesia Haze: Uplifting and Creative

Amnesia Haze is a sativa-dominant strain known for its uplifting and mood-enhancing effects. It is ideal for individuals needing an emotional boost and mental clarity to align with their strategic thinking and creative problem-solving abilities.

- **Effects:** Amnesia Haze delivers a cerebral, euphoric high that enhances mood and energy levels. It helps to reduce stress and anxiety while promoting a positive, optimistic outlook, aligning with the innovative and forward-thinking qualities of Pallas.
- **Flavor and Aroma:** This strain has a citrusy, earthy aroma with hints of sweetness, contributing to its uplifting effects.

- **Usage:** Amnesia Haze is suitable for daytime use, providing a boost in energy and mood without causing sedation, helping individuals stay sharp and engaged in their creative and strategic pursuits.

Conclusion

Pallas, the asteroid symbolizing wisdom and creativity in astrology, represents our capacity for strategic thinking, creative expression, and the integration of intellect and intuition. Understanding its influence can help us harness our innate wisdom, develop our creative talents, and approach challenges with strategic insight. By integrating specific cannabis strains that promote mental clarity, focus, and inspiration, such as Pineapple Express, Sour Tangie, Super Lemon Haze, Jack Herer, and Amnesia Haze, individuals can enhance their natural qualities and maintain their mental sharpness and creativity while engaging in strategic activities. These strains offer a natural way to boost focus, reduce stress, and promote overall well-being, empowering individuals to tap into their wisdom and creativity, fostering growth and innovation. Embracing the influence of Pallas can lead to a life filled with intellectual growth, creative expression, and strategic success.

Check out my Virtual dispensary for all your hemp needs: https://shift.store/sg1fan23477/retail

Chapter 28: Juno: Relationships and Commitment
The Influence of Juno

In astrology, Juno is an asteroid that represents relationships, commitment, and the dynamics of partnerships. Named after the Roman goddess Juno, who was the queen of the gods and the protector of marriage, Juno's placement in our natal chart highlights our attitudes toward relationships, the type of partner we seek, and our approach to commitment. Juno's influence helps us understand the importance of equality, loyalty, and mutual respect in our partnerships.

Key Aspects of Juno in Astrology:

1. **Partnership and Commitment:** Juno represents the themes of partnership and commitment. It influences how we approach long-term relationships and our ability to commit to a partner.
2. **Equality and Balance:** Juno emphasizes the importance of equality and balance in relationships. It highlights our desire for a partnership based on mutual respect and shared responsibilities.
3. **Loyalty and Fidelity:** Juno symbolizes loyalty and fidelity. It reflects our expectations for faithfulness and our own ability to be loyal and devoted in a relationship.
4. **Relationship Dynamics:** Juno sheds light on the dynamics of our relationships, including the challenges and strengths we bring to partnerships. It helps us understand our needs and preferences in a committed relationship.
5. **Influence in the Natal Chart:** The sign and house placement of Juno in an individual's natal chart reveal specific themes and areas of life where partnership and commitment are most influential. It helps us understand the qualities we seek in a partner and the lessons we need to learn about relationships.

Interpreting Juno in Different Signs:

- **Aries Juno:** Seeks an independent and adventurous partner. The relationship needs to be dynamic and stimulating.
- **Taurus Juno:** Seeks a stable and loyal partner. The relationship needs to provide security and comfort.
- **Gemini Juno:** Seeks a communicative and intellectually stimulating partner. The relationship needs to be engaging and mentally enriching.
- **Cancer Juno:** Seeks a nurturing and emotionally supportive partner. The relationship needs to provide a sense of home and belonging.
- **Leo Juno:** Seeks a confident and expressive partner. The relationship needs to be passionate and filled with admiration.
- **Virgo Juno:** Seeks a practical and reliable partner. The relationship needs to be organized and focused on mutual growth.
- **Libra Juno:** Seeks a harmonious and balanced partner. The relationship needs to emphasize equality and mutual respect.
- **Scorpio Juno:** Seeks an intense and transformative partner. The relationship needs to be deep and emotionally connected.
- **Sagittarius Juno:** Seeks an adventurous and freedom-loving partner. The relationship needs to be expansive and filled with shared experiences.
- **Capricorn Juno:** Seeks an ambitious and responsible partner. The relationship needs to be structured and goal-oriented.
- **Aquarius Juno:** Seeks an innovative and independent partner. The relationship needs to be progressive and allow for individuality.
- **Pisces Juno:** Seeks a compassionate and spiritually connected partner. The relationship needs to be empathetic and emotionally fulfilling.

Cannabis Strains for Enhancing Relationships

To support the themes of relationships and commitment represented by Juno, certain cannabis strains can help enhance relaxation, communication, and emotional connection. These strains support the building of strong, loving partnerships by promoting a sense of well-being, reducing stress, and fostering intimacy.

Cherry Pie: Relaxing and Uplifting

Cherry Pie is a hybrid strain known for its balanced effects and sweet, fruity flavor. It is perfect for individuals seeking relaxation and a sense of well-being, enhancing the quality of their relationships.

- **Effects:** Cherry Pie offers a calming, blissful high that helps to reduce stress and promote relaxation. Its balanced effects make it ideal for enhancing feelings of love and connection, fostering a warm and affectionate atmosphere in relationships.
- **Flavor and Aroma:** This strain has a sweet, cherry-like aroma with earthy undertones, contributing to its soothing and enjoyable experience.
- **Usage:** Cherry Pie is suitable for any time of day, providing relaxation and a positive mood that enhances romantic and social interactions, helping individuals build strong, loving partnerships.

Strawberry Cough: Uplifting and Euphoric

Strawberry Cough is a sativa-dominant strain known for its uplifting and euphoric effects. It is an excellent choice for individuals who seek to enhance their mood and social engagement, improving the quality of their relationships.

- **Effects:** Strawberry Cough provides a cerebral, uplifting high that promotes feelings of happiness and well-being. Its euphoric effects can enhance social interactions and create a loving, relaxed environment, aligning with the need for strong and joyful relationships.

- **Flavor and Aroma:** This strain has a sweet, strawberry-like aroma with hints of spice, adding to its delightful sensory experience.
- **Usage:** Strawberry Cough is suitable for daytime use, providing a boost in mood and energy that enhances social and romantic interactions, helping individuals foster loving and joyful partnerships.

Blue Dream: Creative and Uplifting

Blue Dream is a hybrid strain celebrated for its balanced effects that provide both relaxation and mental invigoration. It is an excellent choice for individuals seeking to enhance creativity and emotional connection in their relationships.

- **Effects:** Blue Dream offers a gentle, euphoric high that helps to calm the mind and uplift the spirit. It provides a sense of mental clarity and relaxation without sedation, making it ideal for creative projects and deep conversations.
- **Flavor and Aroma:** This strain has a sweet, berry-like aroma with earthy undertones, contributing to its soothing effects.
- **Usage:** Blue Dream is suitable for any time of day, providing emotional stability and a positive mindset that enhances relationship dynamics, supporting deep and meaningful connections.

Harlequin: Clear-Headed and Focused

Harlequin is a sativa-dominant strain known for its high CBD content and clear-headed effects. It is an excellent choice for individuals seeking mental clarity and focus without intense psychoactive effects during their interactions.

- **Effects:** Harlequin offers a balanced, clear-headed high that enhances focus and concentration. Its high CBD content helps to reduce anxiety and promote mental calmness, making it ideal for nurturing and communicating effectively in relationships.

- **Flavor and Aroma:** This strain has an earthy, woody aroma with hints of mango and citrus, contributing to its refreshing profile.
- **Usage:** Harlequin is suitable for daytime use, providing mental clarity and focus without overwhelming psychoactive effects, helping individuals stay sharp and engaged in their relationships.

ACDC: Clear-Headed and Relaxing

ACDC is a hybrid strain renowned for its high CBD content and minimal psychoactive effects. It is perfect for individuals seeking relaxation and mental clarity without the high.

- **Effects:** ACDC provides a relaxing, clear-headed high that enhances focus and reduces stress. Its high CBD content helps to calm the mind and body, making it suitable for maintaining clear and open communication in relationships.
- **Flavor and Aroma:** This strain has a sweet, earthy aroma with hints of citrus and pine, adding to its calming effects.
- **Usage:** ACDC is best used during the day when mental alertness and relaxation are needed, providing a clear mind and calm demeanor for nurturing and growing relationships.

Conclusion

Juno, the asteroid symbolizing relationships and commitment in astrology, represents our capacity for forming strong partnerships, maintaining loyalty, and fostering mutual respect. Understanding its influence can help us build and sustain loving and balanced relationships. By integrating specific cannabis strains that promote relaxation, mental clarity, and emotional connection, such as Cherry Pie, Strawberry Cough, Blue Dream, Harlequin, and ACDC, individuals can enhance their natural qualities and maintain their emotional well-being while engaging in relationships. These strains offer a natural way to boost focus, reduce stress, and promote overall well-being, empowering individuals to nurture and grow their partnerships, fostering love, commitment, and mutual respect. Embracing the influence of Juno can lead to a life filled with strong, loving relationships and meaningful connections.

Check out my Virtual dispensary for all your hemp needs: https://shift.store/sg1fan23477/retail

Chapter 29: Vesta: Devotion and Focus

The Role of Vesta

In astrology, Vesta is an asteroid that represents devotion, focus, and the sacred flame of inner light and spiritual commitment. Named after the Roman goddess Vesta, who was the goddess of hearth, home, and family, Vesta's placement in our natal chart highlights our dedication to our personal and spiritual goals, our ability to concentrate, and our sense of sacred duty. Vesta's influence helps us understand how we channel our energies towards what we hold sacred and how we maintain focus and commitment in various aspects of our lives.

Key Aspects of Vesta in Astrology:

1. **Devotion and Dedication:** Vesta symbolizes our capacity for devotion and dedication. It influences how we commit to our personal and spiritual goals and the level of dedication we bring to our endeavors.

2. **Focus and Concentration:** Vesta represents our ability to focus and concentrate. It highlights the areas of life where we can achieve a deep sense of concentration and mastery.

3. **Inner Light and Sacred Duty:** Vesta embodies the inner flame of spiritual light and the sense of sacred duty. It reflects our commitment to maintaining our inner light and fulfilling our spiritual responsibilities.

4. **Purity and Integrity:** Vesta is associated with purity and integrity. It emphasizes the importance of maintaining a pure and focused mind, free from distractions and external influences.

5. **Influence in the Natal Chart:** The sign and house placement of Vesta in an individual's natal chart reveal specific themes and areas of life where devotion, focus, and sacred duty are most influential. It helps us understand how we can channel our energies and maintain our inner light.

Interpreting Vesta in Different Signs:

- **Aries Vesta:** Devotion is expressed through action and initiative. Focus comes from embracing new challenges and pioneering ideas.
- **Taurus Vesta:** Devotion is grounded in stability and sensory experiences. Focus comes from creating a secure and comfortable environment.
- **Gemini Vesta:** Devotion is expressed through communication and intellectual pursuits. Focus comes from engaging with diverse ideas and sharing knowledge.
- **Cancer Vesta:** Devotion is nurtured through emotional support and care. Focus comes from fostering a sense of home and belonging.
- **Leo Vesta:** Devotion is expressed through creativity and leadership. Focus comes from inspiring and guiding others with confidence.
- **Virgo Vesta:** Devotion is grounded in practicality and service. Focus comes from maintaining order, health, and efficiency.
- **Libra Vesta:** Devotion is expressed through harmony and balance. Focus comes from fostering relationships and creating beauty.
- **Scorpio Vesta:** Devotion is rooted in transformation and depth. Focus comes from embracing change and exploring hidden truths.
- **Sagittarius Vesta:** Devotion is expressed through exploration and philosophy. Focus comes from seeking knowledge and expanding horizons.
- **Capricorn Vesta:** Devotion is grounded in discipline and responsibility. Focus comes from achieving long-term goals and building lasting success.
- **Aquarius Vesta:** Devotion is expressed through innovation and community. Focus comes from embracing individuality and promoting social progress.

- **Pisces Vesta:** Devotion is nurtured through spirituality and compassion. Focus comes from connecting with the divine and fostering empathy.

Cannabis Strains for Devotion and Focus

To support the themes of devotion and focus represented by Vesta, certain cannabis strains can help enhance mental clarity, concentration, and relaxation. These strains support the ability to maintain focus and dedication to personal and spiritual goals, promoting a sense of inner calm and sacred duty.

OG Kush: Calming and Grounding

OG Kush is a hybrid strain known for its potent relaxing effects and ability to provide a sense of grounding. It is ideal for individuals seeking to reduce stress and enhance focus during their devotional practices.

- **Effects:** OG Kush offers a calming, euphoric high that helps to reduce stress and promote relaxation. Its grounding effects can enhance focus and provide a sense of stability, aligning well with the need for concentration and sacred duty.
- **Flavor and Aroma:** This strain has a complex aroma with notes of earth, pine, and citrus, contributing to its soothing and grounding properties.
- **Usage:** OG Kush is suitable for evening use or during times of high stress, helping individuals unwind and regain emotional balance, facilitating focused and dedicated practices.

Bubba Kush: Calming and Focused

Bubba Kush is an indica strain known for its strong calming effects and ability to promote relaxation. It is perfect for those seeking deep relaxation and mental clarity during their devotional practices.

- **Effects:** Bubba Kush provides a heavy, calming high that promotes deep relaxation and stress relief. Its sedative effects help to reduce anxiety and enhance concentration, making it a perfect complement to introspective and focused activities.

- **Flavor and Aroma:** This strain has a sweet, earthy aroma with hints of coffee and chocolate, adding to its relaxing and grounding profile.
- **Usage:** Bubba Kush is best used in the evening or before bed to promote relaxation and focus, providing a sense of calm and clarity for devotional practices.

Northern Lights: Relaxing and Grounding

Northern Lights is a classic indica strain known for its deeply relaxing and calming effects. It is highly effective for those needing to unwind and achieve emotional tranquility during their devotional practices.

- **Effects:** Northern Lights delivers a potent, body-focused high that promotes relaxation and sleep. Its calming effects help to alleviate stress, anxiety, and emotional tension, making it a perfect strain for grounding and focus.
- **Flavor and Aroma:** This strain has a sweet, earthy aroma with hints of pine and spice, adding to its comforting profile.
- **Usage:** Northern Lights is best used in the evening or before bed to help relax the body and mind, promoting restful sleep and emotional peace, aiding in focused and dedicated practices.

Blue Dream: Creative and Uplifting

Blue Dream is a hybrid strain celebrated for its balanced effects that provide both relaxation and mental invigoration. It is an excellent choice for individuals seeking to enhance creativity and focus during their devotional practices.

- **Effects:** Blue Dream offers a gentle, euphoric high that helps to calm the mind and uplift the spirit. It provides a sense of mental

clarity and relaxation without sedation, making it ideal for creative projects and personal reflection.

- **Flavor and Aroma:** This strain has a sweet, berry-like aroma with earthy undertones, contributing to its soothing effects.
- **Usage:** Blue Dream is suitable for any time of day, providing emotional stability and a positive mindset that enhances focus and devotion.

Harlequin: Clear-Headed and Focused

Harlequin is a sativa-dominant strain known for its high CBD content and clear-headed effects. It is an excellent choice for individuals seeking mental clarity and focus without intense psychoactive effects during their devotional practices.

- **Effects:** Harlequin offers a balanced, clear-headed high that enhances focus and concentration. Its high CBD content helps to reduce anxiety and promote mental calmness, making it ideal for introspection and dedicated activities.
- **Flavor and Aroma:** This strain has an earthy, woody aroma with hints of mango and citrus, contributing to its refreshing profile.
- **Usage:** Harlequin is suitable for daytime use, providing mental clarity and focus without overwhelming psychoactive effects, helping individuals stay sharp and engaged in their devotional practices.

Conclusion

Vesta, the asteroid symbolizing devotion and focus in astrology, represents our capacity for dedication, concentration, and maintaining our inner light. Understanding its influence can help us channel our energies towards personal and spiritual goals, maintaining focus and commitment in various aspects of our lives. By integrating specific cannabis strains that promote mental clarity, concentration, and relaxation, such as OG Kush, Bubba Kush, Northern Lights, Blue Dream, and

Harlequin, individuals can enhance their natural qualities and maintain their emotional well-being while engaging in devotional practices. These strains offer a natural way to boost focus, reduce stress, and promote overall well-being, empowering individuals to nurture their inner light and maintain a sense of sacred duty. Embracing the influence of Vesta can lead to a life filled with dedication, focus, and spiritual fulfillment.

Check out my Virtual dispensary for all your hemp needs: https://shift.store/sg1fan23477/retail

Part IV: Moon Phases and Their Effects

Part IV: Moon Phases and Their Effects

Chapter 30: New Moon: Beginnings and Intention Setting

The Significance of the New Moon

In astrology, the New Moon marks the beginning of a new lunar cycle. It is a time of new beginnings, intention setting, and planting the seeds for future growth. The New Moon occurs when the Sun and Moon are conjunct, meaning they are aligned in the same zodiac sign. This alignment creates a powerful surge of energy that encourages introspection, reflection, and the initiation of new projects and goals. Understanding the significance of the New Moon can help us harness its energy to set intentions and embark on new journeys.

Key Aspects of the New Moon in Astrology:

1. **New Beginnings:** The New Moon represents a fresh start and the opportunity to begin anew. It is a time to release the old and welcome new possibilities.

2. **Intention Setting:** The energy of the New Moon is ideal for setting intentions and goals. It is a powerful time to focus on what we want to manifest in our lives.

3. **Reflection and Introspection:** The New Moon encourages introspection and self-reflection. It is a time to go within and connect with our inner desires and aspirations.

4. **Planting Seeds:** Just as farmers plant seeds during the New Moon to ensure a healthy crop, we can plant the seeds of our intentions and nurture them over the lunar cycle.

5. **Alignment with Zodiac Sign:** The zodiac sign in which the New Moon occurs influences the themes and energies of the intentions we set. Each sign brings its unique qualities and focus areas to the New Moon.

Interpreting the New Moon in Different Signs:

- **Aries New Moon:** Focus on new initiatives, self-assertion, and personal goals. Embrace courage and take action on your desires.
- **Taurus New Moon:** Focus on stability, security, and material well-being. Set intentions related to finances, self-worth, and comfort.
- **Gemini New Moon:** Focus on communication, learning, and social connections. Set intentions related to networking, education, and self-expression.
- **Cancer New Moon:** Focus on home, family, and emotional well-being. Set intentions related to nurturing, self-care, and creating a sense of belonging.
- **Leo New Moon:** Focus on creativity, self-expression, and personal joy. Set intentions related to artistic pursuits, romance, and leadership.
- **Virgo New Moon:** Focus on health, organization, and service. Set intentions related to wellness, daily routines, and practical improvements.
- **Libra New Moon:** Focus on relationships, balance, and harmony. Set intentions related to partnerships, diplomacy, and creating beauty.

- **Scorpio New Moon:** Focus on transformation, deep emotions, and empowerment. Set intentions related to personal growth, healing, and releasing what no longer serves.
- **Sagittarius New Moon:** Focus on adventure, higher learning, and spiritual growth. Set intentions related to travel, education, and expanding horizons.
- **Capricorn New Moon:** Focus on career, ambition, and long-term goals. Set intentions related to professional success, discipline, and structure.
- **Aquarius New Moon:** Focus on innovation, community, and individuality. Set intentions related to social causes, creativity, and embracing uniqueness.
- **Pisces New Moon:** Focus on spirituality, intuition, and compassion. Set intentions related to emotional healing, creativity, and connecting with the divine.

Cannabis Strains for New Beginnings

To support the themes of new beginnings and intention setting represented by the New Moon, certain cannabis strains can help enhance focus, creativity, and relaxation. These strains support the ability to set clear intentions, foster a positive mindset, and embrace new opportunities.

Jack Herer: Creative and Euphoric

Jack Herer is a well-balanced hybrid strain named after the famous cannabis activist. It is known for its potent, clear-headed effects and ability to enhance creativity and concentration.

- **Effects:** Jack Herer offers a blissful, euphoric high that stimulates both the mind and body. It promotes a sense of well-being and encourages creative thinking, making it a perfect complement to the need for mental clarity and focus during the New Moon.

- **Flavor and Aroma:** The strain has a distinctive aroma with notes of pine, earth, and citrus, contributing to its refreshing and energizing effects.
- **Usage:** Jack Herer is often used during creative endeavors or strategic planning activities, providing a burst of energy and inspiration without overwhelming the senses, helping individuals set clear intentions and embrace new beginnings.

Girl Scout Cookies: Uplifting and Relaxing

Girl Scout Cookies (GSC) is a hybrid strain known for its potent effects and delightful flavor. It is perfect for individuals seeking a balance of euphoria and relaxation, enhancing their ability to set intentions and embrace new opportunities.

- **Effects:** Girl Scout Cookies provides a powerful, euphoric high that promotes happiness and relaxation. Its balanced effects help to reduce stress and enhance mood, making it ideal for reflecting on goals and setting new intentions.
- **Flavor and Aroma:** This strain has a sweet, earthy aroma with hints of mint and chocolate, adding to its enjoyable sensory experience.
- **Usage:** Girl Scout Cookies is suitable for any time of day, providing relaxation and a positive mindset that enhances the process of intention setting and embracing new beginnings.

Blue Dream: Creative and Uplifting

Blue Dream is a hybrid strain celebrated for its balanced effects that provide both relaxation and mental invigoration. It is an excellent choice for individuals seeking to enhance creativity and focus during the New Moon.

- **Effects:** Blue Dream offers a gentle, euphoric high that helps to calm the mind and uplift the spirit. It provides a sense of mental

clarity and relaxation without sedation, making it ideal for creative projects and personal reflection.

- **Flavor and Aroma:** This strain has a sweet, berry-like aroma with earthy undertones, contributing to its soothing effects.
- **Usage:** Blue Dream is suitable for any time of day, providing emotional stability and a positive mindset that enhances the process of setting new intentions and embarking on new journeys.

Green Crack: Energizing and Motivating

Green Crack, despite its controversial name, is a pure sativa strain famed for its sharp, invigorating effects. It is perfect for individuals needing a substantial energy boost and mental clarity to embrace new beginnings.

- **Effects:** Green Crack delivers a potent cerebral high that enhances focus, energy, and motivation. Its effects are long-lasting and can help combat stress and fatigue, making it an excellent complement to the New Moon's call for new initiatives and goals.
- **Flavor and Aroma:** This strain has a tangy, fruity flavor reminiscent of mango, with an earthy undertone that adds to its vibrant profile.
- **Usage:** Green Crack is best used during the day when mental alertness and physical activity are required, helping individuals tackle new projects with enthusiasm and vigor.

Sour Diesel: Uplifting and Energizing

Sour Diesel is a sativa-dominant strain known for its fast-acting, energizing effects. It is a popular choice for individuals who seek to enhance vitality and mental clarity during the New Moon.

- **Effects:** Sour Diesel provides an uplifting and euphoric high, making it ideal for combating fatigue and promoting a positive mindset. It can help spark creativity and motivation, aligning well with the New Moon's energy of new beginnings and intention setting.

- **Flavor and Aroma:** This strain has a pungent diesel-like aroma with hints of citrus and earthiness, adding to its invigorating profile.
- **Usage:** Sour Diesel is suitable for daytime use, helping individuals stay active, focused, and inspired throughout the day as they set new intentions and embrace new opportunities.

Conclusion

The New Moon in astrology represents new beginnings, intention setting, and the opportunity to plant the seeds for future growth. Understanding its significance can help us harness its energy to set clear intentions and embark on new journeys. By integrating specific cannabis strains that promote focus, creativity, and relaxation, such as Jack Herer, Girl Scout Cookies, Blue Dream, Green Crack, and Sour Diesel, individuals can enhance their natural qualities and maintain their mental clarity and emotional well-being while engaging in intention setting and embracing new opportunities. These strains offer a natural way to boost focus, reduce stress, and promote overall well-being, empowering individuals to harness the energy of the New Moon and manifest their goals and aspirations. Embracing the influence of the New Moon can lead to a life filled with new beginnings, personal growth, and the fulfillment of our deepest intentions.

Check out my Virtual dispensary for all your hemp needs: https://shift.store/sg1fan23477/retail

Chapter 31: Waxing Crescent: Growth and Momentum
The Influence of the Waxing Crescent

The Waxing Crescent Moon phase occurs immediately after the New Moon, when the Moon starts to show a thin crescent shape. This phase symbolizes growth, momentum, and the gradual build-up of energy towards the Full Moon. During the Waxing Crescent, the intentions set during the New Moon begin to take form, and it is a time for taking action, nurturing new ideas, and building momentum towards achieving our goals.

Key Aspects of the Waxing Crescent in Astrology:

1. **Growth and Expansion:** The Waxing Crescent phase represents growth and expansion. It is a time to cultivate the seeds planted during the New Moon and encourage their development.
2. **Taking Action:** This phase is about taking the first steps toward achieving our goals. It encourages us to take proactive measures and move forward with confidence.
3. **Building Momentum:** The energy of the Waxing Crescent is dynamic and forward-moving. It helps us build momentum and gain traction in our endeavors.
4. **Nurturing Intentions:** The Waxing Crescent is a nurturing phase, where we focus on providing the necessary support and resources for our intentions to grow and flourish.
5. **Increased Motivation:** This phase brings an increase in motivation and enthusiasm. It is an ideal time to focus on projects, set plans into motion, and make tangible progress.

Interpreting the Waxing Crescent in Different Signs:

- **Aries Waxing Crescent:** Focus on initiating new projects and taking bold actions. Embrace courage and drive to push forward with your goals.
- **Taurus Waxing Crescent:** Focus on building stability and nurturing growth. Take practical steps to ensure your plans have a solid foundation.
- **Gemini Waxing Crescent:** Focus on communication and gathering information. Network, learn, and share ideas to support your growth.
- **Cancer Waxing Crescent:** Focus on emotional growth and nurturing relationships. Provide support and care to yourself and others.
- **Leo Waxing Crescent:** Focus on creative expression and self-confidence. Pursue your passions and shine your light.
- **Virgo Waxing Crescent:** Focus on organization and practical improvements. Make detailed plans and take concrete steps to achieve your goals.
- **Libra Waxing Crescent:** Focus on building harmonious relationships and partnerships. Collaborate and seek balance in your endeavors.
- **Scorpio Waxing Crescent:** Focus on transformation and deep emotional work. Embrace change and delve into the depths of your intentions.
- **Sagittarius Waxing Crescent:** Focus on expanding horizons and seeking knowledge. Pursue learning opportunities and adventurous experiences.
- **Capricorn Waxing Crescent:** Focus on career growth and long-term goals. Take disciplined steps to build your success.
- **Aquarius Waxing Crescent:** Focus on innovation and community involvement. Embrace new ideas and work towards progressive change.
- **Pisces Waxing Crescent:** Focus on spiritual growth and creative inspiration. Nurture your inner world and artistic talents.

Cannabis Strains for Growth and Momentum

To support the themes of growth and momentum represented by the Waxing Crescent Moon, certain cannabis strains can help enhance focus, energy, and creativity. These strains support the ability to take proactive steps, build momentum, and nurture new ideas and projects.

Super Lemon Haze: Energizing and Uplifting

Super Lemon Haze is a sativa-dominant hybrid known for its uplifting and energizing effects. It is perfect for individuals seeking a boost in energy and creativity to enhance their growth and momentum.

- **Effects:** Super Lemon Haze provides a cheerful, energetic high that promotes focus, creativity, and motivation. Its uplifting effects help to reduce stress and enhance productivity, aligning with the Waxing Crescent's energy of growth and forward movement.
- **Flavor and Aroma:** This strain has a zesty, citrusy aroma with sweet undertones, adding to its refreshing and invigorating profile.
- **Usage:** Super Lemon Haze is ideal for daytime use, providing a sustained boost in energy and mental sharpness, helping individuals stay active and engaged in their growth-oriented activities.

Blue Dream: Creative and Uplifting

Blue Dream is a hybrid strain celebrated for its balanced effects that provide both relaxation and mental invigoration. It is an excellent choice for individuals seeking to enhance creativity and focus during the Waxing Crescent phase.

- **Effects:** Blue Dream offers a gentle, euphoric high that helps to calm the mind and uplift the spirit. It provides a sense of mental clarity and relaxation without sedation, making it ideal for creative projects and personal growth.
- **Flavor and Aroma:** This strain has a sweet, berry-like aroma with earthy undertones, contributing to its soothing effects.

- **Usage:** Blue Dream is suitable for any time of day, providing emotional stability and a positive mindset that enhances the process of nurturing new ideas and building momentum.

Green Crack: Energizing and Motivating

Green Crack, despite its controversial name, is a pure sativa strain famed for its sharp, invigorating effects. It is perfect for individuals needing a substantial energy boost and mental clarity to build momentum.

- **Effects:** Green Crack delivers a potent cerebral high that enhances focus, energy, and motivation. Its effects are long-lasting and can help combat stress and fatigue, making it an excellent complement to the Waxing Crescent's call for proactive action and growth.
- **Flavor and Aroma:** This strain has a tangy, fruity flavor reminiscent of mango, with an earthy undertone that adds to its vibrant profile.
- **Usage:** Green Crack is best used during the day when mental alertness and physical activity are required, helping individuals tackle new projects with enthusiasm and vigor.

Jack Herer: Creative and Euphoric

Jack Herer is a well-balanced hybrid strain named after the famous cannabis activist. It is known for its potent, clear-headed effects and ability to enhance creativity and concentration.

- **Effects:** Jack Herer offers a blissful, euphoric high that stimulates both the mind and body. It promotes a sense of well-being and encourages creative thinking, making it a perfect complement to the need for mental clarity and focus during the Waxing Crescent phase.

- **Flavor and Aroma:** The strain has a distinctive aroma with notes of pine, earth, and citrus, contributing to its refreshing and energizing effects.
- **Usage:** Jack Herer is often used during creative endeavors or strategic planning activities, providing a burst of energy and inspiration without overwhelming the senses, helping individuals set clear intentions and build momentum.

Pineapple Express: Energizing and Creative

Pineapple Express is a hybrid strain known for its balanced effects, offering both mental stimulation and physical relaxation. It is a favorite for individuals seeking a harmonious blend of energy and calmness to enhance their growth and momentum.

- **Effects:** Pineapple Express provides a mild, euphoric high that promotes happiness and creativity. It enhances focus and productivity while also offering a subtle body relaxation, making it a versatile strain that resonates with the Waxing Crescent's energy of growth and expansion.
- **Flavor and Aroma:** This strain has a delightful tropical aroma with hints of pineapple and citrus, contributing to its refreshing and enjoyable effects.
- **Usage:** Pineapple Express is suitable for any time of day, particularly when a balanced approach to energy and relaxation is desired, helping individuals stay motivated and grounded while engaging in growth-oriented activities.

Conclusion

The Waxing Crescent Moon phase in astrology represents growth, momentum, and the gradual build-up of energy towards the Full Moon. Understanding its significance can help us harness its energy to take proactive steps, nurture new ideas, and build momentum towards achieving our goals. By integrating specific cannabis strains that promote focus, energy, and creativity, such as Super Lemon Haze, Blue Dream, Green Crack, Jack Herer, and Pineapple Express, individuals can enhance their natural qualities and maintain their mental clarity and emotional well-being while engaging in growth-oriented activities. These strains offer a natural way to boost focus, reduce stress, and promote overall well-being, empowering individuals to harness the energy of the Waxing Crescent and achieve their goals with confidence and enthusiasm. Embracing the influence of the Waxing Crescent can lead to a life filled with growth, personal development, and the fulfillment of our intentions.

Check out my Virtual dispensary for all your hemp needs: https://shift.store/sg1fan23477/retail

Chapter 32: First Quarter: Challenges and Decisions
The Impact of the First Quarter

The First Quarter Moon phase occurs approximately one week after the New Moon, when the Moon is half-illuminated and half in shadow. This phase represents a time of challenges, decisions, and action. The energy of the First Quarter Moon is dynamic and assertive, encouraging us to confront obstacles and make necessary decisions to move forward with our intentions. It is a period of testing and refining our goals, where we must overcome resistance and adjust our plans as needed.

Key Aspects of the First Quarter in Astrology:

1. **Confronting Challenges:** The First Quarter Moon brings challenges and obstacles that test our resolve and commitment to our goals. It is a time to face these challenges head-on and find solutions.

2. **Decision-Making:** This phase is about making important decisions and taking decisive action. It encourages us to evaluate our progress and make adjustments to stay on track.

3. **Dynamic Energy:** The energy of the First Quarter Moon is dynamic and assertive. It is a time to be proactive, take initiative, and push through any resistance.

4. **Testing Intentions:** The First Quarter tests the intentions set during the New Moon. It is a period of refining and strengthening our plans, ensuring they are aligned with our true desires.

5. **Building Momentum:** Successfully navigating the First Quarter's challenges helps build momentum and confidence, preparing us for continued growth and progress.

Interpreting the First Quarter in Different Signs:

- **Aries First Quarter:** Focus on taking bold actions and asserting yourself. Overcome challenges through courage and determination.
- **Taurus First Quarter:** Focus on building stability and addressing practical concerns. Overcome challenges through patience and persistence.
- **Gemini First Quarter:** Focus on communication and gathering information. Overcome challenges through adaptability and flexibility.
- **Cancer First Quarter:** Focus on emotional resilience and nurturing relationships. Overcome challenges through empathy and care.
- **Leo First Quarter:** Focus on creative expression and confidence. Overcome challenges through self-assurance and innovation.
- **Virgo First Quarter:** Focus on organization and practical solutions. Overcome challenges through attention to detail and problem-solving.
- **Libra First Quarter:** Focus on balancing relationships and finding harmony. Overcome challenges through diplomacy and cooperation.
- **Scorpio First Quarter:** Focus on transformation and addressing deep-seated issues. Overcome challenges through introspection and emotional strength.
- **Sagittarius First Quarter:** Focus on expanding your horizons and seeking knowledge. Overcome challenges through optimism and open-mindedness.

- **Capricorn First Quarter:** Focus on career goals and long-term planning. Overcome challenges through discipline and strategic thinking.
- **Aquarius First Quarter:** Focus on innovation and social progress. Overcome challenges through creativity and collaboration.
- **Pisces First Quarter:** Focus on spiritual growth and emotional healing. Overcome challenges through compassion and intuition.

Cannabis Strains for Overcoming Challenges

To support the themes of overcoming challenges and making decisions represented by the First Quarter Moon, certain cannabis strains can help enhance focus, energy, and resilience. These strains support the ability to confront obstacles, make clear decisions, and maintain a positive and determined mindset.

Durban Poison: Energizing and Focused

Durban Poison is a pure sativa strain known for its invigorating and uplifting effects. It is ideal for individuals seeking a boost in energy and mental clarity to overcome challenges and make decisive actions.

- **Effects:** Durban Poison provides a powerful, cerebral high that promotes energy, focus, and creativity. Its stimulating effects help to combat fatigue and enhance productivity, aligning with the First Quarter's dynamic energy of action and decision-making.
- **Flavor and Aroma:** This strain has a sweet, earthy aroma with hints of pine and citrus, contributing to its refreshing and invigorating profile.
- **Usage:** Durban Poison is suitable for daytime use, providing a sustained boost in energy and mental sharpness, helping individuals stay active and engaged in their efforts to overcome challenges.

Green Crack: Energizing and Motivating

Green Crack, despite its controversial name, is a pure sativa strain famed for its sharp, invigorating effects. It is perfect for individuals needing a substantial energy boost and mental clarity to navigate the challenges of the First Quarter Moon.

- **Effects:** Green Crack delivers a potent cerebral high that enhances focus, energy, and motivation. Its effects are long-lasting and can help combat stress and fatigue, making it an excellent complement to the First Quarter's call for proactive action and decision-making.
- **Flavor and Aroma:** This strain has a tangy, fruity flavor reminiscent of mango, with an earthy undertone that adds to its vibrant profile.
- **Usage:** Green Crack is best used during the day when mental alertness and physical activity are required, helping individuals tackle challenges with enthusiasm and determination.

Jack Herer: Creative and Euphoric

Jack Herer is a well-balanced hybrid strain named after the famous cannabis activist. It is known for its potent, clear-headed effects and ability to enhance creativity and concentration.

- **Effects:** Jack Herer offers a blissful, euphoric high that stimulates both the mind and body. It promotes a sense of well-being and encourages creative thinking, making it a perfect complement to the need for mental clarity and focus during the First Quarter phase.
- **Flavor and Aroma:** The strain has a distinctive aroma with notes of pine, earth, and citrus, contributing to its refreshing and energizing effects.
- **Usage:** Jack Herer is often used during creative endeavors or strategic planning activities, providing a burst of energy and inspiration without overwhelming the senses, helping individuals set clear intentions and make informed decisions.

Sour Diesel: Uplifting and Energizing

Sour Diesel is a sativa-dominant strain known for its fast-acting, energizing effects. It is a popular choice for individuals who seek to enhance vitality and mental clarity during the First Quarter Moon.

- **Effects:** Sour Diesel provides an uplifting and euphoric high, making it ideal for combating fatigue and promoting a positive mindset. It can help spark creativity and motivation, aligning well with the First Quarter's energy of overcoming challenges and making decisions.
- **Flavor and Aroma:** This strain has a pungent diesel-like aroma with hints of citrus and earthiness, adding to its invigorating profile.
- **Usage:** Sour Diesel is suitable for daytime use, helping individuals stay active, focused, and inspired throughout the day as they navigate challenges and make important decisions.

Super Silver Haze: Creative and Energizing

Super Silver Haze is a sativa-dominant hybrid known for its uplifting and mood-enhancing effects. It is perfect for individuals needing an emotional boost and mental clarity to overcome challenges and make decisive actions.

- **Effects:** Super Silver Haze delivers a cerebral, euphoric high that enhances mood and energy levels. It helps to reduce stress and anxiety while promoting a positive, optimistic outlook, aligning with the First Quarter's dynamic and proactive qualities.
- **Flavor and Aroma:** This strain has a citrusy, earthy aroma with hints of sweetness, contributing to its energizing effects.
- **Usage:** Super Silver Haze is suitable for daytime use, providing a boost in energy and mood without causing sedation, helping individuals stay sharp and engaged in their efforts to overcome challenges and make decisions.

Conclusion

The First Quarter Moon phase in astrology represents challenges, decisions, and the need for dynamic action. Understanding its significance can help us harness its energy to confront obstacles, make important decisions, and build momentum towards achieving our goals. By integrating specific cannabis strains that promote focus, energy, and resilience, such as Durban Poison, Green Crack, Jack Herer, Sour Diesel, and Super Silver Haze, individuals can enhance their natural qualities and maintain their mental clarity and emotional well-being while navigating challenges and making decisions. These strains offer a natural way to boost focus, reduce stress, and promote overall well-being, empowering individuals to harness the energy of the First Quarter Moon and overcome obstacles with confidence and determination. Embracing the influence of the First Quarter Moon can lead to a life filled with personal growth, strategic decisions, and the fulfillment of our intentions.

Check out my Virtual dispensary for all your hemp needs: https://shift.store/sg1fan23477/retail

Chapter 33: Waxing Gibbous: Refinement and Progress
The Role of the Waxing Gibbous

The Waxing Gibbous Moon phase occurs after the First Quarter Moon and leads up to the Full Moon. During this phase, the Moon is more than half illuminated and continues to grow in brightness. The Waxing Gibbous phase represents a time of refinement, progress, and preparation. It is a period where the intentions and actions taken during the New Moon and First Quarter phases are fine-tuned, polished, and brought closer to fruition. This phase encourages us to focus on the details, make necessary adjustments, and ensure that our efforts are aligned with our goals.

Key Aspects of the Waxing Gibbous in Astrology:

1. **Refinement:** The Waxing Gibbous phase is about refining and perfecting our plans and actions. It is a time to focus on the details and make adjustments to ensure everything is on track.

2. **Progress and Growth:** This phase represents significant progress and growth. It is a time to build on the momentum gained during the earlier phases and make substantial strides towards our goals.

3. **Preparation for Fulfillment:** The Waxing Gibbous phase prepares us for the culmination and fulfillment of our intentions during the Full Moon. It is a period of final adjustments and fine-tuning.

4. **Increased Awareness:** During this phase, there is an increased awareness of what needs to be done. It is a time of heightened focus and attention to detail.

5. **Evaluation and Adjustment:** The Waxing Gibbous phase encourages us to evaluate our progress, identify any areas that need improvement, and make necessary adjustments to stay aligned with our goals.

Interpreting the Waxing Gibbous in Different Signs:

- **Aries Waxing Gibbous:** Focus on refining actions and initiatives. Make adjustments to ensure your efforts are bold and effective.
- **Taurus Waxing Gibbous:** Focus on refining stability and material plans. Ensure that your efforts are practical and grounded.
- **Gemini Waxing Gibbous:** Focus on refining communication and information gathering. Make adjustments to ensure clarity and effectiveness in your interactions.
- **Cancer Waxing Gibbous:** Focus on refining emotional connections and nurturing activities. Ensure that your efforts are supportive and caring.
- **Leo Waxing Gibbous:** Focus on refining creative projects and self-expression. Make adjustments to ensure that your efforts shine brightly and confidently.
- **Virgo Waxing Gibbous:** Focus on refining health, organization, and service. Ensure that your efforts are efficient and beneficial.
- **Libra Waxing Gibbous:** Focus on refining relationships and partnerships. Make adjustments to ensure harmony and balance in your interactions.
- **Scorpio Waxing Gibbous:** Focus on refining transformation and deep emotional work. Ensure that your efforts lead to meaningful change and growth.

- **Sagittarius Waxing Gibbous:** Focus on refining knowledge and exploration. Make adjustments to ensure that your efforts expand your horizons and understanding.
- **Capricorn Waxing Gibbous:** Focus on refining career goals and long-term plans. Ensure that your efforts are disciplined and strategic.
- **Aquarius Waxing Gibbous:** Focus on refining innovation and social progress. Make adjustments to ensure that your efforts are forward-thinking and inclusive.
- **Pisces Waxing Gibbous:** Focus on refining spiritual growth and creative inspiration. Ensure that your efforts are compassionate and imaginative.

Cannabis Strains for Refinement and Progress

To support the themes of refinement and progress represented by the Waxing Gibbous Moon, certain cannabis strains can help enhance focus, mental clarity, and relaxation. These strains support the ability to fine-tune plans, make necessary adjustments, and maintain a positive and determined mindset.

Harlequin: Clear-Headed and Focused

Harlequin is a sativa-dominant strain known for its high CBD content and clear-headed effects. It is an excellent choice for individuals seeking mental clarity and focus without intense psychoactive effects during their refinement processes.

- **Effects:** Harlequin offers a balanced, clear-headed high that enhances focus and concentration. Its high CBD content helps to reduce anxiety and promote mental calmness, making it ideal for detailed work and making necessary adjustments.
- **Flavor and Aroma:** This strain has an earthy, woody aroma with hints of mango and citrus, contributing to its refreshing profile.
- **Usage:** Harlequin is suitable for daytime use, providing mental clarity and focus without overwhelming psychoactive effects,

helping individuals stay sharp and engaged in their refinement activities.

ACDC: Clear-Headed and Relaxing

ACDC is a hybrid strain renowned for its high CBD content and minimal psychoactive effects. It is perfect for individuals seeking relaxation and mental clarity without the high, ideal for fine-tuning and progress.

- **Effects:** ACDC provides a relaxing, clear-headed high that enhances focus and reduces stress. Its high CBD content helps to calm the mind and body, making it suitable for tasks requiring attention to detail and composure.
- **Flavor and Aroma:** This strain has a sweet, earthy aroma with hints of citrus and pine, adding to its calming effects.
- **Usage:** ACDC is best used during the day when mental alertness and relaxation are needed, providing a clear mind and calm demeanor for refining and progressing plans.

Blue Dream: Creative and Uplifting

Blue Dream is a hybrid strain celebrated for its balanced effects that provide both relaxation and mental invigoration. It is an excellent choice for individuals seeking to enhance creativity and focus during the Waxing Gibbous phase.

- **Effects:** Blue Dream offers a gentle, euphoric high that helps to calm the mind and uplift the spirit. It provides a sense of mental clarity and relaxation without sedation, making it ideal for creative projects and refining plans.
- **Flavor and Aroma:** This strain has a sweet, berry-like aroma with earthy undertones, contributing to its soothing effects.

- **Usage:** Blue Dream is suitable for any time of day, providing emotional stability and a positive mindset that enhances the process of making progress and refining ideas.

Jack Herer: Creative and Euphoric

Jack Herer is a well-balanced hybrid strain named after the famous cannabis activist. It is known for its potent, clear-headed effects and ability to enhance creativity and concentration.

- **Effects:** Jack Herer offers a blissful, euphoric high that stimulates both the mind and body. It promotes a sense of well-being and encourages creative thinking, making it a perfect complement to the need for mental clarity and focus during the Waxing Gibbous phase.
- **Flavor and Aroma:** The strain has a distinctive aroma with notes of pine, earth, and citrus, contributing to its refreshing and energizing effects.
- **Usage:** Jack Herer is often used during creative endeavors or strategic planning activities, providing a burst of energy and inspiration without overwhelming the senses, helping individuals set clear intentions and make informed decisions.

Pineapple Express: Energizing and Creative

Pineapple Express is a hybrid strain known for its balanced effects, offering both mental stimulation and physical relaxation. It is a favorite for individuals seeking a harmonious blend of energy and calmness to enhance their refinement and progress.

- **Effects:** Pineapple Express provides a mild, euphoric high that promotes happiness and creativity. It enhances focus and productivity while also offering a subtle body relaxation, making it a versatile strain that resonates with the Waxing Gibbous's energy of refinement and growth.

- **Flavor and Aroma:** This strain has a delightful tropical aroma with hints of pineapple and citrus, contributing to its refreshing and enjoyable effects.
- **Usage:** Pineapple Express is suitable for any time of day, particularly when a balanced approach to energy and relaxation is desired, helping individuals stay motivated and grounded while engaging in growth-oriented activities.

Conclusion

The Waxing Gibbous Moon phase in astrology represents refinement, progress, and the preparation for fulfillment. Understanding its significance can help us harness its energy to fine-tune plans, make necessary adjustments, and build momentum towards achieving our goals. By integrating specific cannabis strains that promote focus, mental clarity, and relaxation, such as Harlequin, ACDC, Blue Dream, Jack Herer, and Pineapple Express, individuals can enhance their natural qualities and maintain their mental clarity and emotional well-being while engaging in refinement and progress. These strains offer a natural way to boost focus, reduce stress, and promote overall well-being, empowering individuals to harness the energy of the Waxing Gibbous and make significant strides towards their goals. Embracing the influence of the Waxing Gibbous can lead to a life filled with growth, personal development, and the successful fulfillment of our intentions.

Check out my Virtual dispensary for all your hemp needs: https://shift.store/sg1fan23477/retail

Chapter 34: Full Moon: Culmination and Clarity
The Significance of the Full Moon

The Full Moon is one of the most powerful and significant phases in the lunar cycle. It occurs when the Sun and Moon are in opposition, meaning they are directly opposite each other in the sky, fully illuminating the Moon. The Full Moon represents a time of culmination, clarity, and illumination. It is a period when the intentions set during the New Moon come to fruition, and the results of our efforts become visible. This phase brings heightened emotions, insights, and the potential for significant breakthroughs.

Key Aspects of the Full Moon in Astrology:

1. **Culmination:** The Full Moon signifies the peak of the lunar cycle, a time when projects and intentions reach their culmination. It is a moment of completion and realization.
2. **Clarity and Illumination:** During the Full Moon, everything is illuminated, bringing clarity and insight. Hidden aspects come to light, and we gain a deeper understanding of our situations.
3. **Heightened Emotions:** The energy of the Full Moon amplifies emotions and sensitivities. It is a time when feelings are intensified, and we may experience heightened awareness of our emotional states.
4. **Release and Letting Go:** The Full Moon also marks a time for releasing what no longer serves us. It encourages us to let go of negative patterns, thoughts, and behaviors.

5. **Celebration and Gratitude:** This phase is a time for celebration and gratitude for the progress we have made. It is an opportunity to acknowledge our achievements and appreciate the journey.

Interpreting the Full Moon in Different Signs:

- **Aries Full Moon:** Focus on personal achievements and assertiveness. Gain clarity on your individual goals and take decisive action.
- **Taurus Full Moon:** Focus on material stability and self-worth. Gain clarity on your values and appreciate the abundance in your life.
- **Gemini Full Moon:** Focus on communication and intellectual pursuits. Gain clarity on your ideas and share your knowledge.
- **Cancer Full Moon:** Focus on home, family, and emotional well-being. Gain clarity on your emotional needs and nurture your relationships.
- **Leo Full Moon:** Focus on creativity and self-expression. Gain clarity on your talents and celebrate your unique contributions.
- **Virgo Full Moon:** Focus on health, organization, and service. Gain clarity on your routines and make improvements for better efficiency.
- **Libra Full Moon:** Focus on relationships and harmony. Gain clarity on your partnerships and seek balance in your interactions.
- **Scorpio Full Moon:** Focus on transformation and deep emotional connections. Gain clarity on your inner desires and embrace change.
- **Sagittarius Full Moon:** Focus on exploration and higher learning. Gain clarity on your beliefs and expand your horizons.
- **Capricorn Full Moon:** Focus on career and long-term goals. Gain clarity on your ambitions and celebrate your achievements.

- **Aquarius Full Moon:** Focus on innovation and community involvement. Gain clarity on your social contributions and embrace new ideas.
- **Pisces Full Moon:** Focus on spirituality and compassion. Gain clarity on your spiritual path and connect with your inner self.

Cannabis Strains for Clarity and Culmination

To support the themes of clarity and culmination represented by the Full Moon, certain cannabis strains can help enhance mental clarity, relaxation, and insight. These strains support the ability to gain clear insights, celebrate achievements, and release what no longer serves us.

Blue Dream: Creative and Uplifting

Blue Dream is a hybrid strain celebrated for its balanced effects that provide both relaxation and mental invigoration. It is an excellent choice for individuals seeking to enhance clarity and insight during the Full Moon.

- **Effects:** Blue Dream offers a gentle, euphoric high that helps to calm the mind and uplift the spirit. It provides a sense of mental clarity and relaxation without sedation, making it ideal for reflection and gaining insights.
- **Flavor and Aroma:** This strain has a sweet, berry-like aroma with earthy undertones, contributing to its soothing effects.
- **Usage:** Blue Dream is suitable for any time of day, providing emotional stability and a positive mindset that enhances the process of gaining clarity and celebrating achievements.

Northern Lights: Relaxing and Grounding

Northern Lights is a classic indica strain known for its deeply relaxing and calming effects. It is highly effective for those needing to unwind and achieve emotional tranquility during the Full Moon.

- **Effects:** Northern Lights delivers a potent, body-focused high that promotes relaxation and sleep. Its calming effects help to alleviate stress, anxiety, and emotional tension, making it a perfect strain for grounding and introspection.
- **Flavor and Aroma:** This strain has a sweet, earthy aroma with hints of pine and spice, adding to its comforting profile.
- **Usage:** Northern Lights is best used in the evening or before bed to help relax the body and mind, promoting restful sleep and emotional peace, aiding in the process of reflection and release.

Harlequin: Clear-Headed and Focused

Harlequin is a sativa-dominant strain known for its high CBD content and clear-headed effects. It is an excellent choice for individuals seeking mental clarity and focus without intense psychoactive effects during the Full Moon.

- **Effects:** Harlequin offers a balanced, clear-headed high that enhances focus and concentration. Its high CBD content helps to reduce anxiety and promote mental calmness, making it ideal for introspection and gaining insights.
- **Flavor and Aroma:** This strain has an earthy, woody aroma with hints of mango and citrus, contributing to its refreshing profile.
- **Usage:** Harlequin is suitable for daytime use, providing mental clarity and focus without overwhelming psychoactive effects, helping individuals stay sharp and engaged in their reflective activities.

Jack Herer: Creative and Euphoric

Jack Herer is a well-balanced hybrid strain named after the famous cannabis activist. It is known for its potent, clear-headed effects and ability to enhance creativity and concentration.

- **Effects:** Jack Herer offers a blissful, euphoric high that stimulates both the mind and body. It promotes a sense of well-being and encourages creative thinking, making it a perfect complement to the need for mental clarity and focus during the Full Moon phase.
- **Flavor and Aroma:** The strain has a distinctive aroma with notes of pine, earth, and citrus, contributing to its refreshing and energizing effects.
- **Usage:** Jack Herer is often used during creative endeavors or strategic planning activities, providing a burst of energy and inspiration without overwhelming the senses, helping individuals set clear intentions and make informed decisions.

Lavender: Tranquil and Soothing

Lavender is an indica-dominant strain known for its strong calming and sedative effects. It is ideal for those seeking deep relaxation and enhanced spiritual experiences during the Full Moon.

- **Effects:** Lavender provides a heavy, tranquilizing high that eases the mind and body into a state of deep relaxation. Its calming effects help to quiet the mind and promote a sense of peace, making it perfect for meditation and emotional healing.
- **Flavor and Aroma:** This strain has a floral, lavender-like aroma with hints of herbs and spices, enhancing its soothing properties.
- **Usage:** Lavender is best used in the evening or during spiritual practices to promote relaxation, inner peace, and emotional balance, supporting reflection and the release of what no longer serves us.

Conclusion

The Full Moon in astrology represents culmination, clarity, and the peak of the lunar cycle. Understanding its significance can help us harness its energy to gain insights, celebrate achievements, and release what no longer serves us. By integrating specific cannabis strains that promote mental clarity, relaxation, and insight, such as Blue Dream, Northern Lights, Harlequin, Jack Herer, and Lavender, individuals can enhance their natural qualities and maintain their mental clarity and emotional well-being while engaging in reflection and celebration. These strains offer a natural way to boost focus, reduce stress, and promote overall well-being, empowering individuals to harness the energy of the Full Moon and achieve a deeper understanding of their journey. Embracing the influence of the Full Moon can lead to a life filled with clarity, fulfillment, and the successful realization of our intentions.

Check out my Virtual dispensary for all your hemp needs: https://shift.store/sg1fan23477/retail

Chapter 35: Waning Gibbous: Gratitude and Sharing
The Influence of the Waning Gibbous

The Waning Gibbous Moon phase occurs immediately after the Full Moon and lasts until the Third Quarter Moon. During this phase, the Moon begins to decrease in illumination, symbolizing a time of gratitude, reflection, and sharing. The Waning Gibbous is a period for appreciating the progress made, sharing insights and knowledge gained, and preparing to release what is no longer needed as we move towards the new cycle.

Key Aspects of the Waning Gibbous in Astrology:

1. **Gratitude and Reflection:** The Waning Gibbous phase is a time to reflect on the achievements and experiences of the lunar cycle. It encourages us to express gratitude for the progress made and the lessons learned.

2. **Sharing and Teaching:** This phase is ideal for sharing knowledge, insights, and experiences with others. It is a time to give back, teach, and spread the wisdom gained.

3. **Reevaluation and Adjustment:** The Waning Gibbous invites us to reevaluate our goals and intentions, making adjustments as needed. It is a time to consider what has worked well and what needs to be changed.

4. **Preparation for Release:** As the Moon's light decreases, it symbolizes the beginning of the process of letting go. The Waning

Gibbous prepares us for the upcoming release and renewal phases.

5. **Community and Connection:** This phase emphasizes the importance of community and connection. It encourages us to share our successes and insights with others, fostering a sense of unity and support.

Interpreting the Waning Gibbous in Different Signs:

- **Aries Waning Gibbous:** Focus on sharing personal achievements and inspiring others. Reflect on your leadership and courage.
- **Taurus Waning Gibbous:** Focus on sharing material gains and nurturing stability. Reflect on your values and what you have built.
- **Gemini Waning Gibbous:** Focus on sharing knowledge and communication. Reflect on the information and connections you have made.
- **Cancer Waning Gibbous:** Focus on sharing emotional insights and nurturing relationships. Reflect on the bonds and support you have cultivated.
- **Leo Waning Gibbous:** Focus on sharing creative projects and self-expression. Reflect on your talents and how you have inspired others.
- **Virgo Waning Gibbous:** Focus on sharing practical solutions and health tips. Reflect on the improvements and services you have provided.
- **Libra Waning Gibbous:** Focus on sharing harmony and relationship insights. Reflect on the balance and partnerships you have nurtured.
- **Scorpio Waning Gibbous:** Focus on sharing transformative experiences and deep emotions. Reflect on the changes and growth you have undergone.

- **Sagittarius Waning Gibbous:** Focus on sharing wisdom and adventurous stories. Reflect on the knowledge and experiences you have gained.
- **Capricorn Waning Gibbous:** Focus on sharing career achievements and long-term plans. Reflect on the goals and structures you have built.
- **Aquarius Waning Gibbous:** Focus on sharing innovative ideas and social progress. Reflect on the changes and community efforts you have contributed to.
- **Pisces Waning Gibbous:** Focus on sharing spiritual insights and compassionate acts. Reflect on the empathy and creativity you have expressed.

Cannabis Strains for Gratitude and Sharing

To support the themes of gratitude and sharing represented by the Waning Gibbous Moon, certain cannabis strains can help enhance relaxation, social interaction, and a positive mindset. These strains support the ability to reflect, express gratitude, and share knowledge and experiences with others.

Cherry Pie: Relaxing and Uplifting

Cherry Pie is a hybrid strain known for its balanced effects and sweet, fruity flavor. It is perfect for individuals seeking relaxation and a sense of well-being, enhancing their ability to express gratitude and share with others.

- **Effects:** Cherry Pie offers a calming, blissful high that helps to reduce stress and promote relaxation. Its balanced effects make it ideal for enhancing feelings of gratitude and connection, fostering a warm and affectionate atmosphere for sharing.
- **Flavor and Aroma:** This strain has a sweet, cherry-like aroma with earthy undertones, contributing to its soothing and enjoyable experience.

- **Usage:** Cherry Pie is suitable for any time of day, providing relaxation and a positive mood that enhances social and emotional interactions, helping individuals express gratitude and share their experiences.

Strawberry Cough: Uplifting and Euphoric

Strawberry Cough is a sativa-dominant strain known for its uplifting and euphoric effects. It is an excellent choice for individuals who seek to enhance their mood and social engagement, improving the quality of their interactions and expressions of gratitude.

- **Effects:** Strawberry Cough provides a cerebral, uplifting high that promotes feelings of happiness and well-being. Its euphoric effects can enhance social interactions and create a loving, relaxed environment, aligning with the need for gratitude and sharing.
- **Flavor and Aroma:** This strain has a sweet, strawberry-like aroma with hints of spice, adding to its delightful sensory experience.
- **Usage:** Strawberry Cough is suitable for daytime use, providing a boost in mood and energy that enhances social and emotional interactions, helping individuals share their experiences and express gratitude.

Blue Dream: Creative and Uplifting

Blue Dream is a hybrid strain celebrated for its balanced effects that provide both relaxation and mental invigoration. It is an excellent choice for individuals seeking to enhance creativity and focus during the Waning Gibbous phase.

- **Effects:** Blue Dream offers a gentle, euphoric high that helps to calm the mind and uplift the spirit. It provides a sense of mental clarity and relaxation without sedation, making it ideal for reflecting on achievements and sharing insights.

- **Flavor and Aroma:** This strain has a sweet, berry-like aroma with earthy undertones, contributing to its soothing effects.
- **Usage:** Blue Dream is suitable for any time of day, providing emotional stability and a positive mindset that enhances the process of expressing gratitude and sharing experiences.

Lavender: Tranquil and Soothing

Lavender is an indica-dominant strain known for its strong calming and sedative effects. It is ideal for those seeking deep relaxation and enhanced social experiences during the Waning Gibbous phase.

- **Effects:** Lavender provides a heavy, tranquilizing high that eases the mind and body into a state of deep relaxation. Its calming effects help to quiet the mind and promote a sense of peace, making it perfect for reflection and emotional sharing.
- **Flavor and Aroma:** This strain has a floral, lavender-like aroma with hints of herbs and spices, enhancing its soothing properties.
- **Usage:** Lavender is best used in the evening or during social gatherings to promote relaxation, inner peace, and emotional connection, supporting the expression of gratitude and sharing.

Northern Lights: Relaxing and Grounding

Northern Lights is a classic indica strain known for its deeply relaxing and calming effects. It is highly effective for those needing to unwind and achieve emotional tranquility during the Waning Gibbous phase.

- **Effects:** Northern Lights delivers a potent, body-focused high that promotes relaxation and sleep. Its calming effects help to alleviate stress, anxiety, and emotional tension, making it a perfect strain for grounding and introspection.
- **Flavor and Aroma:** This strain has a sweet, earthy aroma with hints of pine and spice, adding to its comforting profile.

- **Usage:** Northern Lights is best used in the evening or before bed to help relax the body and mind, promoting restful sleep and emotional peace, aiding in the process of reflection and sharing.

Conclusion

The Waning Gibbous Moon phase in astrology represents gratitude, sharing, and the beginning of the process of letting go. Understanding its significance can help us harness its energy to reflect on achievements, express gratitude, and share our knowledge and experiences with others. By integrating specific cannabis strains that promote relaxation, social interaction, and a positive mindset, such as Cherry Pie, Strawberry Cough, Blue Dream, Lavender, and Northern Lights, individuals can enhance their natural qualities and maintain their mental clarity and emotional well-being while engaging in reflection and sharing. These strains offer a natural way to boost focus, reduce stress, and promote overall well-being, empowering individuals to harness the energy of the Waning Gibbous and cultivate a sense of gratitude and connection. Embracing the influence of the Waning Gibbous can lead to a life filled with appreciation, community, and the successful sharing of our insights and experiences.

Check out my Virtual dispensary for all your hemp needs: https://shift.store/sg1fan23477/retail

Chapter 36: Last Quarter: Release and Transformation
The Impact of the Last Quarter

The Last Quarter Moon phase occurs one week after the Full Moon and one week before the New Moon. During this phase, the Moon appears half-illuminated, with the opposite side lit compared to the First Quarter. This phase symbolizes a time of release, transformation, and reassessment. It encourages us to let go of what no longer serves us, reflect on our journey, and prepare for new beginnings. The Last Quarter is a time for introspection, understanding, and clearing out the old to make space for the new.

Key Aspects of the Last Quarter in Astrology:

1. **Release:** The Last Quarter Moon represents a time for letting go. It encourages us to release old patterns, habits, and beliefs that no longer serve our highest good.
2. **Transformation:** This phase symbolizes transformation and change. It is a period for personal growth, allowing us to shed our old selves and embrace new perspectives.
3. **Reassessment:** The Last Quarter is a time for reassessment and evaluation. It allows us to review our progress, understand what worked and what didn't, and make necessary adjustments.
4. **Introspection:** This phase is ideal for introspection and self-examination. It is a time to go within, connect with our inner selves, and gain insights into our journey.
5. **Preparation for Renewal:** The Last Quarter prepares us for the upcoming New Moon and the new cycle. It is a period of clearing out the old to make space for new intentions and beginnings.

Interpreting the Last Quarter in Different Signs:

- **Aries Last Quarter:** Focus on releasing old patterns of self-assertion and impulsiveness. Embrace transformation through mindful action and patience.
- **Taurus Last Quarter:** Focus on releasing material attachments and stubbornness. Embrace transformation through flexibility and letting go.
- **Gemini Last Quarter:** Focus on releasing scattered thoughts and superficial connections. Embrace transformation through deep reflection and meaningful communication.
- **Cancer Last Quarter:** Focus on releasing emotional baggage and overprotectiveness. Embrace transformation through emotional healing and vulnerability.
- **Leo Last Quarter:** Focus on releasing ego-driven behaviors and the need for validation. Embrace transformation through humility and self-awareness.
- **Virgo Last Quarter:** Focus on releasing perfectionism and over-criticism. Embrace transformation through acceptance and compassion.
- **Libra Last Quarter:** Focus on releasing dependency and avoidance of conflict. Embrace transformation through assertiveness and balance.
- **Scorpio Last Quarter:** Focus on releasing control and fear of vulnerability. Embrace transformation through trust and emotional openness.
- **Sagittarius Last Quarter:** Focus on releasing dogmatic beliefs and restlessness. Embrace transformation through grounding and focused intention.
- **Capricorn Last Quarter:** Focus on releasing rigidity and over-ambition. Embrace transformation through flexibility and work-life balance.
- **Aquarius Last Quarter:** Focus on releasing detachment and rebelliousness. Embrace transformation through connection and cooperative effort.

- **Pisces Last Quarter:** Focus on releasing escapism and over-idealism. Embrace transformation through realism and grounded spirituality.

Cannabis Strains for Release and Transformation

To support the themes of release and transformation represented by the Last Quarter Moon, certain cannabis strains can help enhance introspection, emotional release, and personal growth. These strains support the ability to let go, embrace change, and gain deep insights into our journey.

Trainwreck: Energizing and Transformative

Trainwreck is a sativa-dominant hybrid known for its potent, energizing effects and its ability to provide a transformative experience. It is ideal for individuals seeking a boost in energy and clarity to facilitate release and transformation.

- **Effects:** Trainwreck provides a strong, euphoric high that enhances creativity, focus, and motivation. Its uplifting effects help to combat stress and anxiety, making it ideal for emotional release and personal transformation.
- **Flavor and Aroma:** This strain has a pungent, earthy aroma with hints of pine and citrus, contributing to its invigorating profile.
- **Usage:** Trainwreck is suitable for daytime use, providing a sustained boost in energy and mental clarity, helping individuals stay active and engaged in their process of release and transformation.

Gorilla Glue: Calming and Grounding

Gorilla Glue, also known as GG4, is a hybrid strain known for its powerful relaxing effects and its ability to provide a grounding experience. It is perfect for individuals seeking deep relaxation and emotional release.

- **Effects:** Gorilla Glue offers a heavy, calming high that promotes deep relaxation and stress relief. Its strong effects help to alleviate anxiety and emotional tension, making it ideal for introspection and letting go.
- **Flavor and Aroma:** This strain has a distinctive aroma with notes of earth, pine, and chocolate, contributing to its soothing and grounding effects.
- **Usage:** Gorilla Glue is best used in the evening or during times of high stress, helping individuals unwind and achieve emotional peace, facilitating the process of release and transformation.

Lavender: Tranquil and Soothing

Lavender is an indica-dominant strain known for its strong calming and sedative effects. It is ideal for those seeking deep relaxation and enhanced spiritual experiences during the Last Quarter phase.

- **Effects:** Lavender provides a heavy, tranquilizing high that eases the mind and body into a state of deep relaxation. Its calming effects help to quiet the mind and promote a sense of peace, making it perfect for meditation and emotional healing.
- **Flavor and Aroma:** This strain has a floral, lavender-like aroma with hints of herbs and spices, enhancing its soothing properties.
- **Usage:** Lavender is best used in the evening or during spiritual practices to promote relaxation, inner peace, and emotional balance, supporting the process of release and transformation.

Northern Lights: Relaxing and Grounding

Northern Lights is a classic indica strain known for its deeply relaxing and calming effects. It is highly effective for those needing to unwind and achieve emotional tranquility during the Last Quarter phase.

- **Effects:** Northern Lights delivers a potent, body-focused high that promotes relaxation and sleep. Its calming effects help to

alleviate stress, anxiety, and emotional tension, making it a perfect strain for grounding and introspection.

- **Flavor and Aroma:** This strain has a sweet, earthy aroma with hints of pine and spice, adding to its comforting profile.
- **Usage:** Northern Lights is best used in the evening or before bed to help relax the body and mind, promoting restful sleep and emotional peace, aiding in the process of reflection and release.

Blue Dream: Creative and Uplifting

Blue Dream is a hybrid strain celebrated for its balanced effects that provide both relaxation and mental invigoration. It is an excellent choice for individuals seeking to enhance creativity and focus during the Last Quarter phase.

- **Effects:** Blue Dream offers a gentle, euphoric high that helps to calm the mind and uplift the spirit. It provides a sense of mental clarity and relaxation without sedation, making it ideal for creative projects and personal reflection.
- **Flavor and Aroma:** This strain has a sweet, berry-like aroma with earthy undertones, contributing to its soothing effects.
- **Usage:** Blue Dream is suitable for any time of day, providing emotional stability and a positive mindset that enhances the process of release and transformation.

Conclusion

The Last Quarter Moon phase in astrology represents release, transformation, and the reassessment of our journey. Understanding its significance can help us harness its energy to let go of old patterns, embrace change, and prepare for new beginnings. By integrating specific cannabis strains that promote introspection, emotional release, and personal growth, such as Trainwreck, Gorilla Glue, Lavender, Northern Lights, and Blue Dream, individuals can enhance their natural qualities and maintain their mental clarity and emotional well-being while engaging in the process of release and transformation. These strains offer a natural way to boost focus, reduce stress, and promote overall well-being, empowering individuals to harness the energy of the Last Quarter Moon and achieve a deeper understanding of their journey. Embracing the influence of the Last Quarter Moon can lead to a life filled with growth, personal development, and the successful realization of our intentions

Check out my Virtual dispensary for all your hemp needs: https://shift.store/sg1fan23477/retail

Chapter 37: Waning Crescent: Rest and Reflection
The Role of the Waning Crescent

The Waning Crescent Moon phase, also known as the Balsamic Moon, is the final phase of the lunar cycle before the New Moon. During this phase, the Moon is a slim crescent, steadily diminishing in light until it disappears completely at the New Moon. The Waning Crescent symbolizes a time of rest, reflection, and release. It encourages us to slow down, introspect, and prepare for the new beginnings that the upcoming New Moon will bring.

Key Aspects of the Waning Crescent in Astrology:

1. **Rest and Recuperation:** The Waning Crescent is a time for rest and recuperation. It signals a period to slow down, conserve energy, and recover from the efforts of the past lunar cycle.
2. **Reflection:** This phase invites deep reflection and introspection. It is an ideal time to look back on the experiences, lessons, and achievements of the past month.
3. **Release and Letting Go:** The Waning Crescent encourages the release of anything that no longer serves us. It is a time to let go of old patterns, habits, and thoughts, making space for new intentions.
4. **Preparation for New Beginnings:** As the Moon's light diminishes, it prepares us for the upcoming New Moon and a fresh start. It is a period of mental and emotional preparation for setting new intentions.
5. **Spiritual Insight:** This phase offers heightened spiritual awareness and insight. It is a time for meditation, connecting with our inner selves, and exploring our spiritual path.

Interpreting the Waning Crescent in Different Signs:

- **Aries Waning Crescent:** Focus on resting from active pursuits and reflecting on personal growth. Release impulsive tendencies and prepare for new beginnings with mindfulness.
- **Taurus Waning Crescent:** Focus on physical rest and reflecting on material values. Release stubbornness and prepare for new ways to find security and comfort.
- **Gemini Waning Crescent:** Focus on mental rest and reflecting on communication patterns. Release scattered thoughts and prepare for clearer, more focused communication.
- **Cancer Waning Crescent:** Focus on emotional rest and reflecting on familial relationships. Release emotional burdens and prepare for nurturing new connections.
- **Leo Waning Crescent:** Focus on creative rest and reflecting on self-expression. Release ego-driven behaviors and prepare for authentic self-expression.
- **Virgo Waning Crescent:** Focus on physical and mental rest and reflecting on routines. Release perfectionist tendencies and prepare for balanced daily practices.
- **Libra Waning Crescent:** Focus on social rest and reflecting on relationships. Release dependency on others and prepare for balanced, harmonious connections.
- **Scorpio Waning Crescent:** Focus on emotional rest and reflecting on transformation. Release control issues and prepare for deeper emotional insights.
- **Sagittarius Waning Crescent:** Focus on spiritual rest and reflecting on beliefs. Release dogmatic views and prepare for expansive, open-minded thinking.
- **Capricorn Waning Crescent:** Focus on professional rest and reflecting on career goals. Release workaholic tendencies and prepare for balanced ambition.
- **Aquarius Waning Crescent:** Focus on intellectual rest and reflecting on social contributions. Release rebelliousness and prepare for innovative, cooperative efforts.

- **Pisces Waning Crescent:** Focus on spiritual rest and reflecting on empathy and compassion. Release escapist tendencies and prepare for grounded spiritual practices.

Cannabis Strains for Rest and Reflection

To support the themes of rest and reflection represented by the Waning Crescent Moon, certain cannabis strains can help enhance relaxation, introspection, and emotional release. These strains support the ability to slow down, look inward, and prepare for the new beginnings that lie ahead.

Lavender: Tranquil and Soothing

Lavender is an indica-dominant strain known for its strong calming and sedative effects. It is ideal for those seeking deep relaxation and enhanced spiritual experiences during the Waning Crescent phase.

- **Effects:** Lavender provides a heavy, tranquilizing high that eases the mind and body into a state of deep relaxation. Its calming effects help to quiet the mind and promote a sense of peace, making it perfect for meditation and emotional healing.
- **Flavor and Aroma:** This strain has a floral, lavender-like aroma with hints of herbs and spices, enhancing its soothing properties.
- **Usage:** Lavender is best used in the evening or during spiritual practices to promote relaxation, inner peace, and emotional balance, supporting rest and reflection.

Purple Kush: Relaxing and Grounding

Purple Kush is a pure indica strain known for its deeply relaxing and grounding effects. It is perfect for individuals seeking profound rest and introspection during the Waning Crescent phase.

- **Effects:** Purple Kush delivers a powerful, body-focused high that promotes deep relaxation and stress relief. Its sedative effects help to alleviate anxiety and emotional tension, making it ideal for introspective practices and restful sleep.

- **Flavor and Aroma:** This strain has a sweet, earthy aroma with hints of berries and grapes, contributing to its comforting and relaxing profile.
- **Usage:** Purple Kush is best used in the evening or before bed to help relax the body and mind, promoting restful sleep and emotional tranquility, aiding in the process of reflection and release.

Northern Lights: Calming and Grounding

Northern Lights is a classic indica strain known for its deeply relaxing and calming effects. It is highly effective for those needing to unwind and achieve emotional tranquility during the Waning Crescent phase.

- **Effects:** Northern Lights delivers a potent, body-focused high that promotes relaxation and sleep. Its calming effects help to alleviate stress, anxiety, and emotional tension, making it a perfect strain for grounding and introspection.
- **Flavor and Aroma:** This strain has a sweet, earthy aroma with hints of pine and spice, adding to its comforting profile.
- **Usage:** Northern Lights is best used in the evening or before bed to help relax the body and mind, promoting restful sleep and emotional peace, aiding in the process of reflection and release.

Granddaddy Purple: Soothing and Relaxing

Granddaddy Purple (GDP) is an indica strain known for its deeply soothing and relaxing effects. It is highly effective for those seeking rest and introspection during the Waning Crescent phase.

- **Effects:** Granddaddy Purple provides a powerful, calming high that helps to reduce stress and promote relaxation. Its soothing effects make it ideal for introspective practices and restful sleep.

- **Flavor and Aroma:** This strain has a sweet, grape-like aroma with earthy undertones, contributing to its comforting and enjoyable experience.
- **Usage:** Granddaddy Purple is best used in the evening or before bed to promote relaxation and restful sleep, helping individuals achieve a deep sense of peace and tranquility.

Blue Dream: Creative and Uplifting

Blue Dream is a hybrid strain celebrated for its balanced effects that provide both relaxation and mental invigoration. It is an excellent choice for individuals seeking to enhance creativity and focus during the Waning Crescent phase.

- **Effects:** Blue Dream offers a gentle, euphoric high that helps to calm the mind and uplift the spirit. It provides a sense of mental clarity and relaxation without sedation, making it ideal for creative projects and personal reflection.
- **Flavor and Aroma:** This strain has a sweet, berry-like aroma with earthy undertones, contributing to its soothing effects.
- **Usage:** Blue Dream is suitable for any time of day, providing emotional stability and a positive mindset that enhances the process of reflection and preparation for new beginnings.

Conclusion

The Waning Crescent Moon phase in astrology represents rest, reflection, and the preparation for new beginnings. Understanding its significance can help us harness its energy to slow down, introspect, and release what no longer serves us. By integrating specific cannabis strains that promote relaxation, introspection, and emotional release, such as Lavender, Purple Kush, Northern Lights, Granddaddy Purple, and Blue Dream, individuals can enhance their natural qualities and maintain their mental clarity and emotional well-being while engaging in the process of rest and reflection. These strains offer a natural way to boost relaxation, reduce stress, and promote overall well-being, empowering individuals to harness the energy of the Waning Crescent and achieve a deeper understanding of their journey. Embracing the influence of the Waning Crescent Moon can lead to a life filled with rest, renewal, and the successful preparation for new intentions and beginnings.

Check out my Virtual dispensary for all your hemp needs: https://shift.store/sg1fan23477/retail

Part V: Celestial Events and Their Influence

Chapter 38: Solar Eclipses: Powerful Transformations
The Impact of Solar Eclipses

Solar eclipses are some of the most powerful and transformative events in astrology. They occur when the Moon passes between the Earth and the Sun, temporarily obscuring the Sun's light. This celestial event can have profound astrological significance, often acting as a catalyst for major changes, revelations, and new beginnings. Solar eclipses mark a time of intensified energy and potential, where the usual patterns of life are disrupted, creating an opportunity for significant transformation.

Key Aspects of Solar Eclipses in Astrology:

1. **Catalysts for Change:** Solar eclipses often act as powerful catalysts for change. They bring to light issues that need to be addressed and push us out of our comfort zones.

2. **New Beginnings:** These events signify potent new beginnings and the start of new cycles. The energy of a solar eclipse can initiate new projects, relationships, and paths in life.

3. **Revelations:** Solar eclipses can bring sudden insights and revelations. They can uncover hidden truths and provide clarity on situations that have been shrouded in confusion.

4. **Heightened Energy:** The energy during a solar eclipse is highly charged and dynamic. It is a time when the usual flow of energy is disrupted, creating a space for breakthroughs and significant shifts.

5. **Disruption of Patterns:** Solar eclipses can disrupt established patterns and routines. This disruption can be unsettling, but it also creates opportunities for growth and transformation.

Interpreting Solar Eclipses in Different Signs:

- **Aries Solar Eclipse:** Focus on personal initiative and leadership. Embrace new beginnings that require courage and independence.
- **Taurus Solar Eclipse:** Focus on material stability and values. Embrace new financial opportunities and ways to enhance security.
- **Gemini Solar Eclipse:** Focus on communication and intellectual pursuits. Embrace new learning experiences and ways to express ideas.
- **Cancer Solar Eclipse:** Focus on home and family. Embrace new emotional connections and ways to nurture yourself and others.
- **Leo Solar Eclipse:** Focus on creativity and self-expression. Embrace new creative projects and ways to shine your light.
- **Virgo Solar Eclipse:** Focus on health and daily routines. Embrace new habits and ways to improve efficiency and well-being.
- **Libra Solar Eclipse:** Focus on relationships and partnerships. Embrace new connections and ways to create harmony and balance.
- **Scorpio Solar Eclipse:** Focus on transformation and deep emotional connections. Embrace new ways to empower yourself and others.
- **Sagittarius Solar Eclipse:** Focus on adventure and higher learning. Embrace new opportunities for growth and expanding horizons.
- **Capricorn Solar Eclipse:** Focus on career and long-term goals. Embrace new professional opportunities and ways to achieve success.
- **Aquarius Solar Eclipse:** Focus on innovation and social progress. Embrace new ideas and ways to contribute to the community.
- **Pisces Solar Eclipse:** Focus on spirituality and compassion. Embrace new spiritual practices and ways to connect with your inner self.

Cannabis Strains for Powerful Transformations

To support the themes of powerful transformations represented by solar eclipses, certain cannabis strains can help enhance clarity, motivation, and resilience. These strains support the ability to embrace change, gain deep insights, and navigate transformative periods with strength and focus.

Gorilla Glue: Calming and Grounding

Gorilla Glue, also known as GG4, is a hybrid strain known for its powerful relaxing effects and its ability to provide a grounding experience. It is perfect for individuals seeking deep relaxation and emotional release during transformative times.

- **Effects:** Gorilla Glue offers a heavy, calming high that promotes deep relaxation and stress relief. Its strong effects help to alleviate anxiety and emotional tension, making it ideal for introspection and letting go.
- **Flavor and Aroma:** This strain has a distinctive aroma with notes of earth, pine, and chocolate, contributing to its soothing and grounding effects.
- **Usage:** Gorilla Glue is best used in the evening or during times of high stress, helping individuals unwind and achieve emotional peace, facilitating the process of transformation and release.

Trainwreck: Energizing and Transformative

Trainwreck is a sativa-dominant hybrid known for its potent, energizing effects and its ability to provide a transformative experience. It is ideal for individuals seeking a boost in energy and clarity to facilitate powerful transformations.

- **Effects:** Trainwreck provides a strong, euphoric high that enhances creativity, focus, and motivation. Its uplifting effects help to combat stress and anxiety, making it ideal for embracing change and gaining new perspectives.

- **Flavor and Aroma:** This strain has a pungent, earthy aroma with hints of pine and citrus, contributing to its invigorating profile.
- **Usage:** Trainwreck is suitable for daytime use, providing a sustained boost in energy and mental clarity, helping individuals stay active and engaged in their transformative processes.

Lavender: Tranquil and Soothing

Lavender is an indica-dominant strain known for its strong calming and sedative effects. It is ideal for those seeking deep relaxation and enhanced spiritual experiences during transformative periods.

- **Effects:** Lavender provides a heavy, tranquilizing high that eases the mind and body into a state of deep relaxation. Its calming effects help to quiet the mind and promote a sense of peace, making it perfect for meditation and emotional healing.
- **Flavor and Aroma:** This strain has a floral, lavender-like aroma with hints of herbs and spices, enhancing its soothing properties.
- **Usage:** Lavender is best used in the evening or during spiritual practices to promote relaxation, inner peace, and emotional balance, supporting transformation and release.

Northern Lights: Relaxing and Grounding

Northern Lights is a classic indica strain known for its deeply relaxing and calming effects. It is highly effective for those needing to unwind and achieve emotional tranquility during transformative periods.

- **Effects:** Northern Lights delivers a potent, body-focused high that promotes relaxation and sleep. Its calming effects help to alleviate stress, anxiety, and emotional tension, making it a perfect strain for grounding and introspection.
- **Flavor and Aroma:** This strain has a sweet, earthy aroma with hints of pine and spice, adding to its comforting profile.

- **Usage:** Northern Lights is best used in the evening or before bed to help relax the body and mind, promoting restful sleep and emotional peace, aiding in the process of reflection and transformation.

Blue Dream: Creative and Uplifting

Blue Dream is a hybrid strain celebrated for its balanced effects that provide both relaxation and mental invigoration. It is an excellent choice for individuals seeking to enhance creativity and focus during transformative periods.

- **Effects:** Blue Dream offers a gentle, euphoric high that helps to calm the mind and uplift the spirit. It provides a sense of mental clarity and relaxation without sedation, making it ideal for creative projects and personal reflection.
- **Flavor and Aroma:** This strain has a sweet, berry-like aroma with earthy undertones, contributing to its soothing effects.
- **Usage:** Blue Dream is suitable for any time of day, providing emotional stability and a positive mindset that enhances the process of embracing change and gaining new insights.

Conclusion

Solar eclipses in astrology represent powerful transformations, new beginnings, and significant shifts in energy. Understanding their impact can help us harness their energy to embrace change, gain insights, and navigate transformative periods with strength and clarity. By integrating specific cannabis strains that promote relaxation, mental clarity, and emotional release, such as Gorilla Glue, Trainwreck, Lavender, Northern Lights, and Blue Dream, individuals can enhance their natural qualities and maintain their mental clarity and emotional well-being while

engaging in the transformative processes brought on by solar eclipses. These strains offer a natural way to boost focus, reduce stress, and promote overall well-being, empowering individuals to harness the energy of solar eclipses and achieve profound personal growth.

Embracing the influence of solar eclipses can lead to a life filled with powerful transformations, new beginnings, and the successful realization of our highest potential.

Harnessing the Energy of Solar Eclipses: Practical Tips

1. **Set Clear Intentions:** During a solar eclipse, set clear intentions for what you wish to transform in your life. Write them down, meditate on them, and visualize their realization.
2. **Embrace Change:** Be open to the changes that come with a solar eclipse. Understand that disruption is often necessary for growth and transformation.
3. **Reflect and Release:** Use the eclipse energy to reflect on past patterns and behaviors that no longer serve you. Focus on releasing these aspects to make way for new beginnings.
4. **Stay Grounded:** Given the intense energy of solar eclipses, it's important to stay grounded. Engage in grounding practices such as meditation, spending time in nature, or using grounding crystals like hematite or black tourmaline.
5. **Practice Self-Care:** Solar eclipses can be emotionally intense. Prioritize self-care to maintain balance and well-being. This includes getting enough rest, eating well, and engaging in activities that bring you joy and relaxation.
6. **Connect with Your Inner Self:** Use the transformative energy of a solar eclipse to deepen your connection with your inner self. Journaling, meditation, and introspective practices can help you gain insights and clarity.

By understanding and utilizing the powerful energy of solar eclipses, you can facilitate profound transformations in your life, aligning yourself with your true path and potential. Embrace the changes, trust in the process, and allow the eclipse to guide you towards a brighter, more fulfilling future.

Check out my Virtual dispensary for all your hemp needs: https://shift.store/sg1fan23477/retail

Chapter 39: Lunar Eclipses: Emotional Breakthroughs
The Influence of Lunar Eclipses

Lunar eclipses are powerful celestial events that occur when the Earth passes between the Sun and the Moon, casting a shadow on the Moon. These events can have profound astrological significance, often acting as catalysts for emotional breakthroughs, revelations, and the release of deep-seated emotions. Lunar eclipses mark a time of heightened sensitivity, introspection, and transformative emotional experiences.

Key Aspects of Lunar Eclipses in Astrology:

1. **Emotional Breakthroughs:** Lunar eclipses can trigger powerful emotional breakthroughs. They bring suppressed feelings to the surface, providing an opportunity for healing and release.
2. **Revelations:** These events can bring sudden insights and revelations. They can uncover hidden truths and provide clarity on emotional and relational issues.
3. **Release and Letting Go:** Lunar eclipses encourage the release of emotional baggage and old patterns. They create a space for letting go of what no longer serves us, making room for new growth.
4. **Heightened Sensitivity:** The energy during a lunar eclipse is highly charged, often leading to heightened emotional sensitivity. This can be both challenging and enlightening.
5. **Transformation:** Lunar eclipses symbolize significant emotional transformation. They offer a chance to re-evaluate our emotional landscape and make profound changes.

Interpreting Lunar Eclipses in Different Signs:

- **Aries Lunar Eclipse:** Focus on releasing anger and impulsiveness. Embrace emotional breakthroughs through courage and self-awareness.
- **Taurus Lunar Eclipse:** Focus on releasing material attachments and stubbornness. Embrace emotional breakthroughs through security and self-worth.
- **Gemini Lunar Eclipse:** Focus on releasing scattered thoughts and superficial connections. Embrace emotional breakthroughs through meaningful communication.
- **Cancer Lunar Eclipse:** Focus on releasing emotional dependencies and overprotectiveness. Embrace emotional breakthroughs through nurturing and self-care.
- **Leo Lunar Eclipse:** Focus on releasing ego-driven behaviors and the need for validation. Embrace emotional breakthroughs through authentic self-expression.
- **Virgo Lunar Eclipse:** Focus on releasing perfectionism and over-criticism. Embrace emotional breakthroughs through acceptance and compassion.
- **Libra Lunar Eclipse:** Focus on releasing dependency and avoidance of conflict. Embrace emotional breakthroughs through balance and harmonious relationships.
- **Scorpio Lunar Eclipse:** Focus on releasing control and fear of vulnerability. Embrace emotional breakthroughs through trust and emotional openness.
- **Sagittarius Lunar Eclipse:** Focus on releasing dogmatic beliefs and restlessness. Embrace emotional breakthroughs through grounding and inner truth.
- **Capricorn Lunar Eclipse:** Focus on releasing rigidity and over-ambition. Embrace emotional breakthroughs through flexibility and emotional balance.
- **Aquarius Lunar Eclipse:** Focus on releasing detachment and rebelliousness. Embrace emotional breakthroughs through connection and cooperation.

- **Pisces Lunar Eclipse:** Focus on releasing escapism and over-idealism. Embrace emotional breakthroughs through grounded spirituality and empathy.

Cannabis Strains for Emotional Breakthroughs

To support the themes of emotional breakthroughs represented by lunar eclipses, certain cannabis strains can help enhance introspection, emotional release, and mental clarity. These strains support the ability to process emotions, gain deep insights, and navigate transformative periods with strength and focus.

Blue Dream: Creative and Uplifting

Blue Dream is a hybrid strain celebrated for its balanced effects that provide both relaxation and mental invigoration. It is an excellent choice for individuals seeking to enhance creativity and emotional clarity during lunar eclipses.

- **Effects:** Blue Dream offers a gentle, euphoric high that helps to calm the mind and uplift the spirit. It provides a sense of mental clarity and relaxation without sedation, making it ideal for processing emotions and gaining insights.
- **Flavor and Aroma:** This strain has a sweet, berry-like aroma with earthy undertones, contributing to its soothing effects.
- **Usage:** Blue Dream is suitable for any time of day, providing emotional stability and a positive mindset that enhances the process of emotional breakthroughs and introspection.

Northern Lights: Relaxing and Grounding

Northern Lights is a classic indica strain known for its deeply relaxing and calming effects. It is highly effective for those needing to unwind and achieve emotional tranquility during lunar eclipses.

- **Effects:** Northern Lights delivers a potent, body-focused high that promotes relaxation and sleep. Its calming effects help to

alleviate stress, anxiety, and emotional tension, making it a perfect strain for grounding and emotional release.

- **Flavor and Aroma:** This strain has a sweet, earthy aroma with hints of pine and spice, adding to its comforting profile.
- **Usage:** Northern Lights is best used in the evening or before bed to help relax the body and mind, promoting restful sleep and emotional peace, aiding in the process of reflection and release.

Lavender: Tranquil and Soothing

Lavender is an indica-dominant strain known for its strong calming and sedative effects. It is ideal for those seeking deep relaxation and enhanced spiritual experiences during transformative periods.

- **Effects:** Lavender provides a heavy, tranquilizing high that eases the mind and body into a state of deep relaxation. Its calming effects help to quiet the mind and promote a sense of peace, making it perfect for meditation and emotional healing.
- **Flavor and Aroma:** This strain has a floral, lavender-like aroma with hints of herbs and spices, enhancing its soothing properties.
- **Usage:** Lavender is best used in the evening or during spiritual practices to promote relaxation, inner peace, and emotional balance, supporting transformation and release.

Granddaddy Purple: Soothing and Relaxing

Granddaddy Purple (GDP) is an indica strain known for its deeply soothing and relaxing effects. It is highly effective for those seeking rest and introspection during the Waning Crescent phase.

- **Effects:** Granddaddy Purple provides a powerful, calming high that helps to reduce stress and promote relaxation. Its soothing effects make it ideal for introspective practices and restful sleep.

- **Flavor and Aroma:** This strain has a sweet, grape-like aroma with earthy undertones, contributing to its comforting and enjoyable experience.
- **Usage:** Granddaddy Purple is best used in the evening or before bed to promote relaxation and restful sleep, helping individuals achieve a deep sense of peace and tranquility.

Trainwreck: Energizing and Transformative

Trainwreck is a sativa-dominant hybrid known for its potent, energizing effects and its ability to provide a transformative experience. It is ideal for individuals seeking a boost in energy and clarity to facilitate emotional breakthroughs.

- **Effects:** Trainwreck provides a strong, euphoric high that enhances creativity, focus, and motivation. Its uplifting effects help to combat stress and anxiety, making it ideal for processing emotions and gaining new perspectives.
- **Flavor and Aroma:** This strain has a pungent, earthy aroma with hints of pine and citrus, contributing to its invigorating profile.
- **Usage:** Trainwreck is suitable for daytime use, providing a sustained boost in energy and mental clarity, helping individuals stay active and engaged in their emotional processing.

Conclusion

Lunar eclipses in astrology represent emotional breakthroughs, revelations, and significant shifts in our emotional landscape. Understanding their impact can help us harness their energy to process emotions, gain insights, and navigate transformative periods with strength and clarity. By integrating specific cannabis strains that promote relaxation, mental clarity, and emotional release, such as Blue Dream, Northern Lights, Lavender, Granddaddy Purple, and Trainwreck, individuals can enhance their natural qualities and maintain their mental clarity and emotional well-being while engaging in the process of emotional breakthroughs. These strains offer a natural way to boost focus, reduce stress, and promote overall well-being, empowering individuals to harness the energy of lunar eclipses and achieve profound personal growth.

Embracing the influence of lunar eclipses can lead to a life filled with emotional clarity, healing, and the successful realization of our deepest emotional truths.

Check out my Virtual dispensary for all your hemp needs: https://shift.store/sg1fan23477/retail

Chapter 40: Planetary Retrogrades: Reflection and Reassessment

The Role of Planetary Retrogrades

In astrology, planetary retrogrades occur when a planet appears to move backward in its orbit from our perspective on Earth. This optical illusion is caused by the relative positions and motions of Earth and the other planets in the solar system. While the planets do not actually move backward, their apparent retrograde motion has significant astrological implications. Retrogrades are times of reflection, reassessment, and revision, where the energies of the planets are turned inward, encouraging introspection and reevaluation.

Key Aspects of Planetary Retrogrades in Astrology:

1. **Reflection:** Retrograde periods are ideal for introspection and reflection. They encourage us to look back on our past actions, decisions, and experiences to gain deeper understanding and insights.
2. **Reassessment:** During retrogrades, we are invited to reassess our goals, plans, and strategies. This is a time to evaluate what is working and what needs to be adjusted.
3. **Revision:** Retrogrades offer an opportunity to revise and refine our projects and ideas. It is a period to make necessary changes and improvements.
4. **Delays and Disruptions:** Retrogrades can bring delays and disruptions, which can be frustrating but also provide valuable lessons in patience and resilience.
5. **Inner Work:** The inward focus of retrogrades encourages inner work and personal growth. It is a time to connect with our inner selves and address unresolved issues.

Interpreting Different Planetary Retrogrades:

- **Mercury Retrograde:** Focus on communication, travel, and technology. This period is known for misunderstandings, delays, and technical glitches. It is an ideal time for reviewing and revising plans, reconnecting with old friends, and resolving past issues.
- **Venus Retrograde:** Focus on relationships, love, and finances. This period encourages us to reevaluate our relationships and financial matters, reconnect with past lovers, and reassess our values.
- **Mars Retrograde:** Focus on energy, motivation, and conflict. This period can bring frustrations and a lack of motivation. It is a time to reassess our goals, re-evaluate how we use our energy, and address unresolved conflicts.
- **Jupiter Retrograde:** Focus on growth, expansion, and philosophy. This period encourages us to re-evaluate our beliefs, reassess our goals for growth, and review our plans for personal and professional expansion.
- **Saturn Retrograde:** Focus on structure, discipline, and responsibilities. This period is a time to review our long-term goals, reassess our commitments, and address areas where we need to build stronger foundations.
- **Uranus Retrograde:** Focus on innovation, change, and freedom. This period encourages us to reassess our desire for change, review innovative ideas, and address areas where we feel restricted.
- **Neptune Retrograde:** Focus on spirituality, dreams, and illusions. This period is a time for spiritual reflection, reassessing our dreams, and addressing areas where we may be deceiving ourselves or others.
- **Pluto Retrograde:** Focus on transformation, power, and control. This period encourages deep introspection, addressing issues of power and control, and embracing personal transformation.

Cannabis Strains for Reflection and Reassessment

To support the themes of reflection and reassessment represented by planetary retrogrades, certain cannabis strains can help enhance introspection, relaxation, and mental clarity. These strains support the ability to look inward, gain insights, and navigate periods of reevaluation with calm and focus.

OG Kush: Calming and Grounding

OG Kush is a hybrid strain known for its powerful relaxing effects and its ability to provide a grounding experience. It is ideal for individuals seeking deep relaxation and mental clarity during periods of reflection and reassessment.

- **Effects:** OG Kush offers a calming, euphoric high that helps to reduce stress and promote relaxation. Its grounding effects can enhance focus and provide a sense of stability, aligning well with the need for introspection and reassessment.
- **Flavor and Aroma:** This strain has a complex aroma with notes of earth, pine, and citrus, contributing to its soothing and grounding properties.
- **Usage:** OG Kush is suitable for evening use or during times of high stress, helping individuals unwind and regain emotional balance, facilitating deep reflection and reassessment.

Bubba Kush: Relaxing and Focused

Bubba Kush is an indica strain known for its strong calming effects and ability to promote deep relaxation. It is perfect for those seeking mental clarity and focus during periods of reflection and reassessment.

- **Effects:** Bubba Kush provides a heavy, calming high that promotes deep relaxation and stress relief. Its sedative effects help to reduce anxiety and enhance concentration, making it ideal for introspective practices and mental clarity.

- **Flavor and Aroma:** This strain has a sweet, earthy aroma with hints of coffee and chocolate, adding to its relaxing and grounding profile.
- **Usage:** Bubba Kush is best used in the evening or before bed to promote relaxation and restful sleep, helping individuals achieve a state of calm and focus for reflection and reassessment.

Harlequin: Clear-Headed and Focused

Harlequin is a sativa-dominant strain known for its high CBD content and clear-headed effects. It is an excellent choice for individuals seeking mental clarity and focus without intense psychoactive effects during periods of reflection and reassessment.

- **Effects:** Harlequin offers a balanced, clear-headed high that enhances focus and concentration. Its high CBD content helps to reduce anxiety and promote mental calmness, making it ideal for introspection and gaining insights.
- **Flavor and Aroma:** This strain has an earthy, woody aroma with hints of mango and citrus, contributing to its refreshing profile.
- **Usage:** Harlequin is suitable for daytime use, providing mental clarity and focus without overwhelming psychoactive effects, helping individuals stay sharp and engaged in their reflective activities.

Northern Lights: Relaxing and Grounding

Northern Lights is a classic indica strain known for its deeply relaxing and calming effects. It is highly effective for those needing to unwind and achieve emotional tranquility during periods of reflection and reassessment.

- **Effects:** Northern Lights delivers a potent, body-focused high that promotes relaxation and sleep. Its calming effects help to

alleviate stress, anxiety, and emotional tension, making it a perfect strain for grounding and introspection.

- **Flavor and Aroma:** This strain has a sweet, earthy aroma with hints of pine and spice, adding to its comforting profile.
- **Usage:** Northern Lights is best used in the evening or before bed to help relax the body and mind, promoting restful sleep and emotional peace, aiding in the process of reflection and reassessment.

Blue Dream: Creative and Uplifting

Blue Dream is a hybrid strain celebrated for its balanced effects that provide both relaxation and mental invigoration. It is an excellent choice for individuals seeking to enhance creativity and focus during periods of reflection and reassessment.

- **Effects:** Blue Dream offers a gentle, euphoric high that helps to calm the mind and uplift the spirit. It provides a sense of mental clarity and relaxation without sedation, making it ideal for creative projects and personal reflection.
- **Flavor and Aroma:** This strain has a sweet, berry-like aroma with earthy undertones, contributing to its soothing effects.
- **Usage:** Blue Dream is suitable for any time of day, providing emotional stability and a positive mindset that enhances the process of reflection and reassessment.

Conclusion

Planetary retrogrades in astrology represent periods of reflection, reassessment, and revision. Understanding their impact can help us harness their energy to look inward, gain insights, and navigate periods of reevaluation with calm and focus. By integrating specific cannabis strains that promote relaxation, mental clarity, and introspection, such as OG Kush, Bubba Kush, Harlequin, Northern Lights, and Blue Dream, individuals can enhance their natural qualities and maintain their mental clarity and emotional well-being while engaging in the process of reflection and reassessment. These strains offer a natural way to boost focus, reduce stress, and promote overall well-being, empowering individuals to harness the energy of planetary retrogrades and achieve profound personal growth.

Embracing the influence of planetary retrogrades can lead to a life filled with deeper understanding, emotional clarity, and the successful realization of our highest potential.

Check out my Virtual dispensary for all your hemp needs: https://shift.store/sg1fan23477/retail

Chapter 41: Meteor Showers: Inspiration and Creativity

The Impact of Meteor Showers

Meteor showers, often viewed as spectacular celestial events, occur when Earth passes through the trail of debris left by a comet. As these small particles enter Earth's atmosphere, they burn up, creating streaks of light known as meteors or "shooting stars." In astrology, meteor showers are seen as harbingers of inspiration, creativity, and sudden insights. These events can stimulate our imagination and open our minds to new possibilities, acting as catalysts for creative expression and innovative thinking.

Key Aspects of Meteor Showers in Astrology:

1. **Inspiration:** Meteor showers are associated with bursts of inspiration. They can ignite our creativity and provide fresh ideas, helping us see things from new perspectives.
2. **Creativity:** These celestial events stimulate creative energy, making them an ideal time for artistic pursuits, writing, brainstorming, and problem-solving.
3. **Sudden Insights:** Meteor showers can bring sudden insights and revelations. They can help us connect the dots in ways we hadn't considered before, leading to breakthrough moments.
4. **Renewed Energy:** The dynamic energy of meteor showers can refresh our minds and spirits, providing a boost in motivation and enthusiasm for our projects and goals.
5. **Spiritual Significance:** Meteor showers are often seen as messages from the universe, encouraging us to pay attention to our dreams and intuition, and to follow our creative impulses.

Interpreting Meteor Showers in Different Signs:

- **Aries Meteor Shower:** Focus on igniting personal projects and pioneering ideas. Embrace inspiration through action and leadership.
- **Taurus Meteor Shower:** Focus on creative projects related to beauty, nature, and material well-being. Embrace inspiration through stability and sensuality.
- **Gemini Meteor Shower:** Focus on writing, communication, and intellectual pursuits. Embrace inspiration through curiosity and social interaction.
- **Cancer Meteor Shower:** Focus on home-based projects and emotional expression. Embrace inspiration through nurturing and connecting with family.
- **Leo Meteor Shower:** Focus on artistic endeavors and self-expression. Embrace inspiration through confidence and creative flair.
- **Virgo Meteor Shower:** Focus on practical creativity and problem-solving. Embrace inspiration through organization and attention to detail.
- **Libra Meteor Shower:** Focus on creative partnerships and harmony. Embrace inspiration through collaboration and balance.
- **Scorpio Meteor Shower:** Focus on transformative and deep creative projects. Embrace inspiration through intensity and emotional depth.
- **Sagittarius Meteor Shower:** Focus on exploring new creative horizons and philosophical ideas. Embrace inspiration through adventure and learning.
- **Capricorn Meteor Shower:** Focus on structured and disciplined creative projects. Embrace inspiration through ambition and long-term planning.
- **Aquarius Meteor Shower:** Focus on innovative and unconventional creative ideas. Embrace inspiration through originality and social progress.

- **Pisces Meteor Shower:** Focus on spiritual and artistic expression. Embrace inspiration through imagination and empathy.

Cannabis Strains for Inspiration and Creativity

To support the themes of inspiration and creativity represented by meteor showers, certain cannabis strains can help enhance mental clarity, focus, and creative thinking. These strains support the ability to tap into creative energies, gain fresh insights, and explore new ideas with enthusiasm and innovation.

Pineapple Express: Energizing and Creative

Pineapple Express is a hybrid strain known for its balanced effects, offering both mental stimulation and physical relaxation. It is perfect for individuals seeking a harmonious blend of energy and calmness to enhance their creativity.

- **Effects:** Pineapple Express provides a mild, euphoric high that promotes happiness and creativity. It enhances focus and productivity while also offering a subtle body relaxation, making it a versatile strain that resonates with the dynamic energy of meteor showers.
- **Flavor and Aroma:** This strain has a delightful tropical aroma with hints of pineapple and citrus, contributing to its refreshing and enjoyable effects.
- **Usage:** Pineapple Express is suitable for any time of day, particularly when a balanced approach to energy and relaxation is desired, helping individuals stay motivated and grounded while engaging in creative activities.

Sour Tangie: Energizing and Uplifting

Sour Tangie is a sativa-dominant hybrid known for its uplifting and energizing effects. It is an excellent choice for individuals seeking a boost in energy and creativity to facilitate innovative thinking and inspiration.

- **Effects:** Sour Tangie provides a powerful, cerebral high that enhances focus, creativity, and motivation. Its uplifting effects help to combat stress and promote a positive mindset, making it ideal for brainstorming sessions and creative projects.
- **Flavor and Aroma:** This strain has a tangy, citrusy flavor with earthy undertones, contributing to its invigorating profile.
- **Usage:** Sour Tangie is suitable for daytime use, providing a sustained boost in energy and mental clarity, helping individuals stay active and engaged in their creative endeavors.

Blue Dream: Creative and Uplifting

Blue Dream is a hybrid strain celebrated for its balanced effects that provide both relaxation and mental invigoration. It is an excellent choice for individuals seeking to enhance creativity and focus during periods of inspiration.

- **Effects:** Blue Dream offers a gentle, euphoric high that helps to calm the mind and uplift the spirit. It provides a sense of mental clarity and relaxation without sedation, making it ideal for creative projects and personal reflection.
- **Flavor and Aroma:** This strain has a sweet, berry-like aroma with earthy undertones, contributing to its soothing effects.
- **Usage:** Blue Dream is suitable for any time of day, providing emotional stability and a positive mindset that enhances the process of gaining new insights and exploring creative ideas.

Green Crack: Energizing and Motivating

Green Crack, despite its controversial name, is a pure sativa strain famed for its sharp, invigorating effects. It is perfect for individuals needing a substantial energy boost and mental clarity to embrace inspiration and creativity.

- **Effects:** Green Crack delivers a potent cerebral high that enhances focus, energy, and motivation. Its effects are long-lasting and can help combat stress and fatigue, making it an excellent complement to the need for dynamic and innovative thinking.
- **Flavor and Aroma:** This strain has a tangy, fruity flavor reminiscent of mango, with an earthy undertone that adds to its vibrant profile.
- **Usage:** Green Crack is best used during the day when mental alertness and physical activity are required, helping individuals tackle creative projects with enthusiasm and vigor.

Harlequin: Clear-Headed and Focused

Harlequin is a sativa-dominant strain known for its high CBD content and clear-headed effects. It is an excellent choice for individuals seeking mental clarity and focus without intense psychoactive effects during periods of inspiration.

- **Effects:** Harlequin offers a balanced, clear-headed high that enhances focus and concentration. Its high CBD content helps to reduce anxiety and promote mental calmness, making it ideal for creative thinking and problem-solving.
- **Flavor and Aroma:** This strain has an earthy, woody aroma with hints of mango and citrus, contributing to its refreshing profile.
- **Usage:** Harlequin is suitable for daytime use, providing mental clarity and focus without overwhelming psychoactive effects, helping individuals stay sharp and engaged in their creative processes.

Conclusion

Meteor showers in astrology represent bursts of inspiration, creativity, and sudden insights. Understanding their impact can help us harness their energy to tap into our creative potential, gain fresh ideas, and explore new possibilities with enthusiasm and innovation. By integrating specific cannabis strains that promote mental clarity, focus, and creative thinking, such as Pineapple Express, Sour Tangie, Blue Dream, Green Crack, and Harlequin, individuals can enhance their natural qualities and maintain their mental clarity and emotional well-being while engaging in creative activities. These strains offer a natural way to boost focus, reduce stress, and promote overall well-being, empowering individuals to harness the energy of meteor showers and achieve profound creative expression.

Embracing the influence of meteor showers can lead to a life filled with inspiration, creativity, and the successful realization of our most imaginative ideas.

Check out my Virtual dispensary for all your hemp needs: https://shift.store/sg1fan23477/retail

Chapter 42: Solar Flares: Energy Surges
The Influence of Solar Flares

Solar flares are powerful bursts of radiation and energy emitted from the Sun's surface. These flares can have significant impacts on Earth, affecting communication systems, power grids, and even human behavior. In astrology, solar flares are seen as intense energy surges that can influence our physical and mental states, often leading to heightened alertness, increased motivation, and a boost in energy levels. They can also bring about sudden shifts and changes, making them times of both opportunity and challenge.

Key Aspects of Solar Flares in Astrology:

1. **Energy Surges:** Solar flares bring intense energy surges that can lead to increased motivation and productivity. They can act as a powerful catalyst for action and change.
2. **Heightened Alertness:** The energy from solar flares can heighten our senses and make us more alert. This increased awareness can help us to react quickly to new situations and opportunities.
3. **Sudden Shifts:** Solar flares can bring about sudden shifts and changes in our lives. These shifts can be both challenging and exciting, pushing us out of our comfort zones.
4. **Enhanced Creativity:** The intense energy can also stimulate creativity and innovative thinking, making it a great time for brainstorming and exploring new ideas.
5. **Physical and Mental Effects:** Solar flares can have physical and mental effects, such as restlessness, anxiety, or difficulty sleeping. It is important to find ways to manage these effects and harness the energy positively.

Interpreting Solar Flares in Different Signs:

- **Aries Solar Flares:** Focus on harnessing energy for personal projects and leadership. Embrace the surge of motivation to initiate new ventures.
- **Taurus Solar Flares:** Focus on using the energy to enhance material stability and comfort. Channel the increased motivation into practical and financial goals.
- **Gemini Solar Flares:** Focus on communication and intellectual pursuits. Use the heightened alertness to absorb new information and share ideas.
- **Cancer Solar Flares:** Focus on emotional connections and home projects. Utilize the energy to nurture relationships and create a supportive environment.
- **Leo Solar Flares:** Focus on creative expression and self-confidence. Harness the energy surge to showcase your talents and inspire others.
- **Virgo Solar Flares:** Focus on organization and health. Use the heightened awareness to improve daily routines and enhance well-being.
- **Libra Solar Flares:** Focus on relationships and harmony. Channel the energy into building balanced and supportive partnerships.
- **Scorpio Solar Flares:** Focus on transformation and deep emotional work. Use the intense energy to make significant changes and embrace personal growth.
- **Sagittarius Solar Flares:** Focus on exploration and learning. Utilize the energy surge to expand your horizons and pursue new adventures.
- **Capricorn Solar Flares:** Focus on career goals and long-term plans. Harness the motivation to achieve professional success and build strong foundations.
- **Aquarius Solar Flares:** Focus on innovation and social progress. Use the heightened alertness to contribute to community projects and embrace new ideas.

- **Pisces Solar Flares:** Focus on spirituality and creativity. Channel the intense energy into artistic endeavors and spiritual practices.

Cannabis Strains for Harnessing Energy

To support the themes of energy surges represented by solar flares, certain cannabis strains can help enhance focus, motivation, and physical energy. These strains support the ability to harness the intense energy, stay productive, and manage any restlessness or anxiety that may arise.

Durban Poison: Energizing and Focused

Durban Poison is a pure sativa strain known for its invigorating and uplifting effects. It is ideal for individuals seeking a boost in energy and mental clarity to harness the dynamic energy of solar flares.

- **Effects:** Durban Poison provides a powerful, cerebral high that promotes energy, focus, and creativity. Its stimulating effects help to combat fatigue and enhance productivity, making it ideal for periods of heightened alertness and motivation.
- **Flavor and Aroma:** This strain has a sweet, earthy aroma with hints of pine and citrus, contributing to its refreshing and energizing profile.
- **Usage:** Durban Poison is suitable for daytime use, providing a sustained boost in energy and mental sharpness, helping individuals stay active and engaged in their pursuits.

Green Crack: Energizing and Motivating

Green Crack, despite its controversial name, is a pure sativa strain famed for its sharp, invigorating effects. It is perfect for individuals needing a substantial energy boost and mental clarity to harness the intense energy of solar flares.

- **Effects:** Green Crack delivers a potent cerebral high that enhances focus, energy, and motivation. Its effects are long-lasting and can help combat stress and fatigue, making it an excellent complement to the need for dynamic and innovative thinking.

- **Flavor and Aroma:** This strain has a tangy, fruity flavor reminiscent of mango, with an earthy undertone that adds to its vibrant profile.
- **Usage:** Green Crack is best used during the day when mental alertness and physical activity are required, helping individuals tackle new projects and opportunities with enthusiasm and vigor.

Sour Diesel: Uplifting and Energizing

Sour Diesel is a sativa-dominant strain known for its fast-acting, energizing effects. It is a popular choice for individuals who seek to enhance vitality and mental clarity during periods of heightened energy.

- **Effects:** Sour Diesel provides an uplifting and euphoric high, making it ideal for combating fatigue and promoting a positive mindset. It can help spark creativity and motivation, aligning well with the dynamic energy of solar flares.
- **Flavor and Aroma:** This strain has a pungent diesel-like aroma with hints of citrus and earthiness, adding to its invigorating profile.
- **Usage:** Sour Diesel is suitable for daytime use, helping individuals stay active, focused, and inspired throughout the day as they harness the energy surges of solar flares.

Jack Herer: Creative and Euphoric

Jack Herer is a well-balanced hybrid strain named after the famous cannabis activist. It is known for its potent, clear-headed effects and ability to enhance creativity and concentration.

- **Effects:** Jack Herer offers a blissful, euphoric high that stimulates both the mind and body. It promotes a sense of well-being and encourages creative thinking, making it a perfect complement to the need for mental clarity and focus during periods of heightened energy.

- **Flavor and Aroma:** The strain has a distinctive aroma with notes of pine, earth, and citrus, contributing to its refreshing and energizing effects.
- **Usage:** Jack Herer is often used during creative endeavors or strategic planning activities, providing a burst of energy and inspiration without overwhelming the senses, helping individuals stay productive and engaged.

Pineapple Express: Energizing and Creative

Pineapple Express is a hybrid strain known for its balanced effects, offering both mental stimulation and physical relaxation. It is perfect for individuals seeking a harmonious blend of energy and calmness to enhance their creativity and productivity.

- **Effects:** Pineapple Express provides a mild, euphoric high that promotes happiness and creativity. It enhances focus and productivity while also offering a subtle body relaxation, making it a versatile strain that resonates with the dynamic energy of solar flares.
- **Flavor and Aroma:** This strain has a delightful tropical aroma with hints of pineapple and citrus, contributing to its refreshing and enjoyable effects.
- **Usage:** Pineapple Express is suitable for any time of day, particularly when a balanced approach to energy and relaxation is desired, helping individuals stay motivated and grounded while engaging in creative activities.

Conclusion

Solar flares in astrology represent powerful energy surges, heightened alertness, and opportunities for dynamic change and innovation. Understanding their impact can help us harness their energy to stay motivated, productive, and creative. By integrating specific cannabis strains that promote focus, energy, and mental clarity, such as Durban Poison, Green Crack, Sour Diesel, Jack Herer, and Pineapple Express, individuals can enhance their natural qualities and maintain their mental clarity and emotional well-being while engaging in productive activities. These strains offer a natural way to boost focus, reduce stress, and promote overall well-being, empowering individuals to harness the energy of solar flares and achieve profound personal and professional growth.

Embracing the influence of solar flares can lead to a life filled with increased energy, creativity, and the successful realization of our most ambitious goals and projects.

Check out my Virtual dispensary for all your hemp needs: https://shift.store/sg1fan23477/retail

Chapter 43: Comets: Signs and Omens
The Significance of Comets in Astrology

Comets have long been regarded as powerful celestial phenomena, often associated with significant events, changes, and transformations. In astrology, comets are seen as messengers, bringing signs and omens that can indicate major shifts in our lives and in the world. The appearance of a comet is rare and dramatic, symbolizing sudden insights, revelations, and the need to pay attention to important messages from the universe.

Key Aspects of Comets in Astrology:

1. **Harbingers of Change:** Comets are often seen as harbingers of change, signaling the end of an era and the beginning of a new one. They bring the energy of transformation and upheaval.

2. **Messengers of Revelation:** Comets can bring sudden insights and revelations. They act as catalysts for awakening, urging us to pay attention to signs and messages that may otherwise go unnoticed.

3. **Omens and Portents:** Historically, comets have been interpreted as omens, indicating significant events or shifts in the collective consciousness. They are often seen as precursors to important changes on a personal and global scale.

4. **Heightened Awareness:** The appearance of a comet can heighten our awareness and intuition. It encourages us to look beyond the ordinary and explore deeper meanings and connections.

5. **Spiritual Significance:** Comets are often associated with spiritual growth and enlightenment. They can inspire us to connect with our higher selves and embrace a broader perspective on life.

Interpreting Comets in Different Signs:

- **Aries Comet:** Focus on initiating bold changes and embracing new beginnings. Pay attention to signs that encourage personal growth and leadership.
- **Taurus Comet:** Focus on transformations related to material stability and values. Look for omens that suggest shifts in your financial or material circumstances.
- **Gemini Comet:** Focus on changes in communication and intellectual pursuits. Be open to revelations that inspire new ways of thinking and expressing yourself.
- **Cancer Comet:** Focus on transformations in home and family life. Look for signs that encourage emotional growth and nurturing connections.
- **Leo Comet:** Focus on creative expression and self-confidence. Pay attention to omens that inspire you to shine and share your talents with the world.
- **Virgo Comet:** Focus on changes in health and daily routines. Be open to insights that inspire new ways to improve your well-being and efficiency.
- **Libra Comet:** Focus on transformations in relationships and partnerships. Look for signs that encourage balance and harmony in your interactions.
- **Scorpio Comet:** Focus on deep emotional and psychological changes. Pay attention to omens that inspire profound inner transformation and empowerment.
- **Sagittarius Comet:** Focus on exploring new horizons and expanding your knowledge. Be open to signs that encourage adventure and philosophical growth.
- **Capricorn Comet:** Focus on career and long-term goals. Look for omens that inspire you to reassess your ambitions and strategies for success.

- **Aquarius Comet:** Focus on innovation and social progress. Pay attention to signs that inspire new ways to contribute to the collective good.
- **Pisces Comet:** Focus on spiritual growth and creative inspiration. Be open to revelations that inspire deeper connections with your intuition and artistic expression.

Cannabis Strains for Interpreting Signs and Omens

To support the themes of interpreting signs and omens represented by comets, certain cannabis strains can help enhance intuition, mental clarity, and spiritual awareness. These strains support the ability to tune into subtle messages, gain insights, and explore deeper meanings and connections.

Harlequin: Clear-Headed and Focused

Harlequin is a sativa-dominant strain known for its high CBD content and clear-headed effects. It is an excellent choice for individuals seeking mental clarity and focus while interpreting signs and omens.

- **Effects:** Harlequin offers a balanced, clear-headed high that enhances focus and concentration. Its high CBD content helps to reduce anxiety and promote mental calmness, making it ideal for introspection and gaining insights.
- **Flavor and Aroma:** This strain has an earthy, woody aroma with hints of mango and citrus, contributing to its refreshing profile.
- **Usage:** Harlequin is suitable for daytime use, providing mental clarity and focus without overwhelming psychoactive effects, helping individuals stay sharp and engaged in their reflective activities.

ACDC: Clear-Headed and Relaxing

ACDC is a hybrid strain renowned for its high CBD content and minimal psychoactive effects. It is perfect for individuals seeking relaxation and mental clarity while interpreting signs and omens.

- **Effects:** ACDC provides a relaxing, clear-headed high that enhances focus and reduces stress. Its high CBD content helps to calm the mind and body, making it suitable for tasks requiring attention to detail and introspection.
- **Flavor and Aroma:** This strain has a sweet, earthy aroma with hints of citrus and pine, adding to its calming effects.
- **Usage:** ACDC is best used during the day when mental alertness and relaxation are needed, providing a clear mind and calm demeanor for interpreting signs and gaining insights.

Northern Lights: Relaxing and Grounding

Northern Lights is a classic indica strain known for its deeply relaxing and calming effects. It is highly effective for those needing to unwind and achieve emotional tranquility while interpreting signs and omens.

- **Effects:** Northern Lights delivers a potent, body-focused high that promotes relaxation and sleep. Its calming effects help to alleviate stress, anxiety, and emotional tension, making it a perfect strain for grounding and introspection.
- **Flavor and Aroma:** This strain has a sweet, earthy aroma with hints of pine and spice, adding to its comforting profile.
- **Usage:** Northern Lights is best used in the evening or before bed to help relax the body and mind, promoting restful sleep and emotional peace, aiding in the process of reflection and interpretation.

Lavender: Tranquil and Soothing

Lavender is an indica-dominant strain known for its strong calming and sedative effects. It is ideal for those seeking deep relaxation and enhanced spiritual experiences during periods of interpreting signs and omens.

- **Effects:** Lavender provides a heavy, tranquilizing high that eases the mind and body into a state of deep relaxation. Its calming effects help to quiet the mind and promote a sense of peace, making it perfect for meditation and emotional healing.
- **Flavor and Aroma:** This strain has a floral, lavender-like aroma with hints of herbs and spices, enhancing its soothing properties.
- **Usage:** Lavender is best used in the evening or during spiritual practices to promote relaxation, inner peace, and emotional balance, supporting reflection and interpretation.

Blue Dream: Creative and Uplifting

Blue Dream is a hybrid strain celebrated for its balanced effects that provide both relaxation and mental invigoration. It is an excellent choice for individuals seeking to enhance creativity and focus during periods of interpreting signs and omens.

- **Effects:** Blue Dream offers a gentle, euphoric high that helps to calm the mind and uplift the spirit. It provides a sense of mental clarity and relaxation without sedation, making it ideal for creative projects and personal reflection.
- **Flavor and Aroma:** This strain has a sweet, berry-like aroma with earthy undertones, contributing to its soothing effects.
- **Usage:** Blue Dream is suitable for any time of day, providing emotional stability and a positive mindset that enhances the process of gaining new insights and exploring creative ideas.

Conclusion

Comets in astrology represent powerful signs and omens, bringing messages of change, revelation, and transformation. Understanding their significance can help us harness their energy to interpret important messages, gain insights, and embrace new perspectives. By integrating specific cannabis strains that promote mental clarity, focus, and spiritual awareness, such as Harlequin, ACDC, Northern Lights, Lavender, and Blue Dream, individuals can enhance their natural qualities and maintain their mental clarity and emotional well-being while interpreting signs and omens. These strains offer a natural way to boost focus, reduce stress, and promote overall well-being, empowering individuals to harness the energy of comets and achieve profound personal and spiritual growth.

Check out my Virtual dispensary for all your hemp needs: https://shift.store/sg1fan23477/retail

Part VI: Conclusion and Appendices

Chapter 44: Conclusion: Integrating Astrological Insights and Cannabis Use

Recap of Key Concepts

Throughout **Zodiacal Herbage: Astrological Insights: Cannabis Universe: Volume 2,** we have explored the profound connections between astrology and cannabis, delving into how celestial events and astrological influences can be complemented by the mindful use of cannabis strains. Here's a recap of the key concepts covered:

1. **Astrological Influences:** We examined how each planet, moon phase, and celestial event (such as solar and lunar eclipses, meteor showers, and solar flares) affects our lives. Each astrological influence brings unique energies and opportunities for personal growth, transformation, and reflection.

2. **Zodiac Signs and Cannabis:** We explored the traits and characteristics of each zodiac sign and identified cannabis strains that enhance these qualities or provide balance. Each sign benefits from different strains that cater to its specific needs for relaxation, focus, creativity, or emotional support.

3. **Moon Phases:** We looked at the significance of each moon phase, from the New Moon's beginnings to the Full Moon's culmination and the Waning Crescent's reflection. Cannabis strains were recommended to align with the energies of each phase, helping individuals navigate these cyclical influences.

4. **Celestial Events:** Special attention was given to events like solar and lunar eclipses, meteor showers, and solar flares. These powerful occurrences were linked to cannabis strains that help

harness their dynamic energies for transformation, creativity, and insight.

5. **Planetary Retrogrades:** We discussed the reflective and re-assessing nature of planetary retrogrades, recommending strains that support introspection, relaxation, and mental clarity during these times.

Practical Tips for Integrating Astrology and Cannabis

Integrating astrological insights with mindful cannabis use can enhance your overall well-being, deepen your understanding of yourself, and help you navigate life's challenges and opportunities more effectively. Here are some practical tips for integrating astrology and cannabis into your daily life:

1. **Know Your Chart:** Start by understanding your natal chart. Identify your sun, moon, and rising signs, as well as the positions of other key planets. This knowledge will help you tailor your cannabis use to your unique astrological profile.

2. **Follow the Moon Phases:** Align your cannabis use with the lunar cycle. Use strains that support new beginnings and intention-setting during the New Moon, strains that promote clarity and culmination during the Full Moon, and strains that aid in reflection and release during the Waning Moon phases.

3. **Monitor Planetary Transits:** Keep track of significant planetary transits and retrogrades. During retrogrades, use strains that enhance introspection and mental clarity. For powerful transits like conjunctions or oppositions, choose strains that help you stay grounded and focused.

4. **Personalized Strain Selection:** Choose cannabis strains that complement your zodiac sign's traits and needs. For example, if you are a Leo, strains like Pineapple Express or Sour Diesel can enhance your creativity and self-expression. If you are a Taurus,

strains like Granddaddy Purple or Northern Lights can provide the stability and relaxation you crave.

5. **Set Intentions:** Use cannabis intentionally by setting specific goals or intentions before consumption. Whether you seek creativity, relaxation, or spiritual insight, clear intentions can help guide your experience and make it more meaningful.

6. **Mindful Consumption:** Practice mindfulness during cannabis use. Pay attention to how different strains affect your mood, energy levels, and overall well-being. Adjust your consumption based on your astrological influences and personal needs.

7. **Create Rituals:** Incorporate cannabis into your astrological rituals. Use it during meditation, journaling, or other reflective practices to deepen your connection with yourself and the universe. Create a calming environment with music, candles, and other elements that enhance your experience.

8. **Track Your Experiences:** Keep a journal to record your experiences with different strains and astrological influences. Note how specific strains affect you during various moon phases, planetary transits, and other celestial events. This can help you fine-tune your cannabis use for maximum benefit.

9. **Stay Informed:** Continuously educate yourself about both astrology and cannabis. Follow reputable sources, join online communities, and stay updated on new research and insights. This ongoing learning will enhance your ability to integrate these practices effectively.

10. **Balance and Moderation:** Always practice balance and moderation in your cannabis use. Pay attention to how much and how often you consume, ensuring it supports your overall health and well-being.

Integrating Astrology and Cannabis for Holistic Well-being

The integration of astrological insights and mindful cannabis use offers a unique path to holistic well-being. By aligning your cannabis consumption with the natural rhythms and energies of the cosmos, you can enhance your physical, emotional, and spiritual health. This approach encourages you to live in harmony with the universe, making conscious choices that support your growth and transformation.

As you continue your journey with astrology and cannabis, remember that both practices are deeply personal and should be tailored to your individual needs and experiences. Embrace the insights and opportunities they offer, and use them as tools for self-discovery, healing, and empowerment. With mindful intention and a deeper understanding of the cosmic forces at play, you can navigate life's challenges and opportunities with grace, wisdom, and a heightened sense of purpose.

Thank you for exploring **Zodiacal Herbage: Astrological Insights: Cannabis Universe: Volume 2**. May your journey with astrology and cannabis be enlightening, transformative, and filled with profound insights and joyful experiences.

Appendices
Appendix A: Glossary of Cannabis Strains
This glossary provides definitions and descriptions of the cannabis strains discussed in **Zodiacal Herbage: Astrological Insights: Cannabis Universe: Volume 2**. Each strain has unique characteristics and effects that can complement various astrological influences and personal needs.

ACDC

- **Type:** Hybrid (High-CBD)
- **Effects:** Clear-headed, relaxing, minimal psychoactive effects
- **Flavor and Aroma:** Sweet, earthy, citrus
- **Usage:** Ideal for daytime use, promoting mental clarity and reducing anxiety without significant psychoactive effects. Great for introspection and focus during planetary retrogrades and for interpreting signs and omens.

Blue Dream

- **Type:** Hybrid
- **Effects:** Uplifting, creative, relaxing
- **Flavor and Aroma:** Sweet, berry-like, earthy
- **Usage:** Suitable for any time of day, providing a gentle, euphoric high that enhances creativity and mental clarity. Perfect for Full Moon activities and moments of inspiration.

Bubba Kush

- **Type:** Indica

- **Effects:** Deep relaxation, stress relief, sedative
- **Flavor and Aroma:** Sweet, earthy, coffee, chocolate
- **Usage:** Best used in the evening or before bed for deep relaxation and stress relief. Ideal for reflection and reassessment during planetary retrogrades.

Cherry Pie

- **Type:** Hybrid
- **Effects:** Relaxing, uplifting, euphoric
- **Flavor and Aroma:** Sweet, cherry-like, earthy
- **Usage:** Suitable for any time of day, enhancing social interactions and promoting a positive mood. Great for expressing gratitude and sharing during the Waning Gibbous phase.

Durban Poison

- **Type:** Sativa
- **Effects:** Energizing, uplifting, focused
- **Flavor and Aroma:** Sweet, earthy, pine, citrus
- **Usage:** Ideal for daytime use, providing a sustained boost in energy and mental sharpness. Excellent for harnessing energy surges during solar flares and for tackling new projects.

Gorilla Glue (GG4)

- **Type:** Hybrid
- **Effects:** Relaxing, euphoric, grounding
- **Flavor and Aroma:** Earthy, pine, chocolate
- **Usage:** Best used in the evening or during times of high stress for deep relaxation and emotional release. Perfect for facilitating powerful transformations during solar eclipses.

Granddaddy Purple (GDP)

- **Type:** Indica
- **Effects:** Soothing, relaxing, euphoric
- **Flavor and Aroma:** Sweet, grape-like, earthy
- **Usage:** Ideal for evening use, promoting deep relaxation and restful sleep. Suitable for rest and introspection during the Waning Crescent phase.

Green Crack

- **Type:** Sativa
- **Effects:** Energizing, motivating, focused
- **Flavor and Aroma:** Tangy, fruity, earthy
- **Usage:** Best used during the day for a substantial boost in energy and mental clarity. Great for dynamic thinking and productivity during solar flares and meteor showers.

Harlequin

- **Type:** Sativa-dominant (High-CBD)
- **Effects:** Clear-headed, focused, minimal psychoactive effects
- **Flavor and Aroma:** Earthy, woody, mango, citrus
- **Usage:** Suitable for daytime use, enhancing focus and reducing anxiety without significant psychoactive effects. Excellent for interpreting signs and omens and for reflection during planetary retrogrades.

Jack Herer

- **Type:** Hybrid
- **Effects:** Creative, euphoric, clear-headed
- **Flavor and Aroma:** Pine, earth, citrus

- **Usage:** Ideal for creative endeavors and strategic planning. Provides a burst of energy and inspiration, making it perfect for solar flares and moments requiring mental clarity.

Lavender

- **Type:** Indica
- **Effects:** Tranquil, sedative, relaxing
- **Flavor and Aroma:** Floral, lavender, herbal, spicy
- **Usage:** Best used in the evening or during spiritual practices for deep relaxation and emotional healing. Suitable for periods of transformation and reflection.

Northern Lights

- **Type:** Indica
- **Effects:** Calming, relaxing, sleep-inducing
- **Flavor and Aroma:** Sweet, earthy, pine, spice
- **Usage:** Ideal for evening use or before bed to promote relaxation and restful sleep. Great for grounding and introspection during reflective periods.

OG Kush

- **Type:** Hybrid
- **Effects:** Relaxing, euphoric, grounding
- **Flavor and Aroma:** Earthy, pine, citrus
- **Usage:** Suitable for evening use or during times of high stress for relaxation and mental clarity. Perfect for periods of reassessment and introspection.

Pineapple Express

- **Type:** Hybrid
- **Effects:** Energizing, creative, uplifting
- **Flavor and Aroma:** Tropical, pineapple, citrus
- **Usage:** Suitable for any time of day, providing a harmonious blend of energy and calmness. Excellent for creative activities and moments of inspiration.

Sour Diesel

- **Type:** Sativa-dominant
- **Effects:** Uplifting, energizing, creative
- **Flavor and Aroma:** Pungent, diesel, citrus, earthy
- **Usage:** Ideal for daytime use, providing a boost in energy and mental clarity. Perfect for periods of dynamic change and innovative thinking.

Sour Tangie

- **Type:** Sativa-dominant
- **Effects:** Energizing, uplifting, creative
- **Flavor and Aroma:** Tangy, citrus, earthy
- **Usage:** Suitable for daytime use, providing sustained energy and mental clarity. Great for brainstorming and creative endeavors during meteor showers.

Strawberry Cough

- **Type:** Sativa-dominant
- **Effects:** Uplifting, euphoric, creative
- **Flavor and Aroma:** Sweet, strawberry, spice
- **Usage:** Suitable for daytime use, enhancing mood and creativity. Ideal for social interactions and sharing experiences.

Trainwreck

- **Type:** Sativa-dominant
- **Effects:** Energizing, creative, transformative
- **Flavor and Aroma:** Earthy, pine, citrus
- **Usage:** Best used during the day for a boost in energy and clarity. Excellent for embracing powerful transformations and sudden insights.

This glossary provides a comprehensive overview of the cannabis strains discussed in **Zodiacal Herbage: Astrological Insights: Cannabis Universe: Volume 2**. Each strain has unique properties that can enhance your astrological journey, helping you align with celestial energies and navigate life's challenges and opportunities with greater ease and awareness.

Appendix B: Astrological Charts and Tables

This appendix provides a comprehensive set of charts and tables for quick reference on planetary positions, moon phases, and celestial events. These resources are designed to help you easily navigate and integrate astrological insights into your daily life and cannabis use.

Planetary Positions

Understanding the current positions of the planets is essential for interpreting their influences on your life. The following table provides a snapshot of the planets' positions and their significance.

Planet	Sign	Duration in Sign	Key Influences
Sun	Varies	~30 days	Vitality, self-expression, identity
Moon	Varies	~2.5 days	Emotions, intuition, inner life
Mercury	Varies	~15-60 days	Communication, intellect, travel
Venus	Varies	~23-60 days	Love, beauty, relationships
Mars	Varies	~45-60 days	Energy, action, aggression
Jupiter	Varies	~1 year	Growth, expansion, luck

Saturn	Varies	~2.5 years	Discipline, responsibility, structure
Uranus	Varies	~7 years	Innovation, change, rebellion
Neptune	Varies	~14 years	Dreams, spirituality, illusions
Pluto	Varies	~12-31 years	Transformation, power, regeneration

Moon Phases

The lunar cycle influences our emotions, behaviors, and energy levels. Use the following chart to understand the moon phases and their corresponding energies.

Moon Phase	Duration	Key Influences	Recommended Strains
New Moon	1-2 days	New beginnings, intention setting	Jack Herer, Girl Scout Cookies
Waxing Crescent	~7 days	Growth, momentum, action	Super Lemon Haze, Blue Dream
First Quarter	1-2 days	Challenges, decisions, overcoming obstacles	Durban Poison, Green Crack

Waxing Gibbous	~7 days	Refinement, progress, preparation	Harlequin, ACDC
Full Moon	1-2 days	Culmination, clarity, illumination	Blue Dream, Northern Lights
Waning Gibbous	~7 days	Gratitude, sharing, reevaluation	Cherry Pie, Strawberry Cough
Last Quarter	1-2 days	Release, transformation, letting go	Trainwreck, Gorilla Glue
Waning Crescent	~7 days	Rest, reflection, preparation for new cycle	Lavender, Purple Kush

Celestial Events

Celestial events like solar and lunar eclipses, meteor showers, and solar flares have significant astrological impacts. Refer to the following table for quick insights into these events and their influences.

Celestial Event	Frequency	Key Influences	Recommended Strains
Solar Eclipse	2-4 times per year	Powerful transformations, new beginnings	Gorilla Glue, Trainwreck
Lunar Eclipse	2-4 times per year	Emotional breakthroughs, revelations	Blue Dream, Northern Lights

| Meteor Shower | Several times per year | Inspiration, creativity, sudden insights | Pineapple Express, Sour Tangie |
| Solar Flare | Sporadic | Energy surges, heightened alertness | Durban Poison, Green Crack |

Retrogrades

Planetary retrogrades encourage reflection and reassessment. The following chart provides a quick reference to the retrograde periods of key planets and their influences.

Planet	Retrograde Frequency	Duration	Key Influences	Recommended Strains
Mercury	3-4 times per year	~3 weeks	Communication issues, travel delays, revisiting past	Harlequin, ACDC
Venus	Every 18 months	~6 weeks	Reevaluation of relationships, finances	Cherry Pie, Lavender
Mars	Every 2 years	~2.5 months	Reduced motivation, reassessment of goals	OG Kush, Bubba Kush

Jupiter	Annually	~4 months	Reevaluation of growth, philosophical beliefs	Blue Dream, Northern Lights
Saturn	Annually	~4.5 months	Reevaluation of responsibilities, structures	Granddaddy Purple, Lavender
Uranus	Annually	~5 months	Reevaluation of innovation, social changes	Pineapple Express, Harlequin
Neptune	Annually	~5-6 months	Reevaluation of dreams, spirituality	Northern Lights, ACDC
Pluto	Annually	~5-6 months	Deep transformation, power dynamics	Gorilla Glue, Trainwreck

Utilizing Astrological Charts and Tables

To make the most of these charts and tables:

1. **Plan Ahead:** Use the planetary positions chart to understand the current astrological climate and plan your activities accordingly. Align your goals and actions with the energies of the planets.
2. **Follow the Moon:** Track the moon phases to sync your activities with the lunar cycle. Use the recommended strains to enhance your experience during each phase.

3. **Observe Celestial Events:** Mark your calendar with upcoming celestial events. Use the suggested strains to harness their powerful energies for personal growth and transformation.

4. **Navigate Retrogrades:** Be mindful of retrograde periods and their potential impacts. Use the recommended strains to support introspection and reassessment during these times.

5. **Keep a Journal:** Document your experiences with different strains and astrological influences. This will help you fine-tune your approach and better understand how to integrate astrology and cannabis into your life.

By using these charts and tables, you can easily reference and integrate astrological insights and cannabis use into your daily routine, enhancing your overall well-being and aligning with the natural rhythms of the universe.

Appendix C: Recommended Reading and Resources

This appendix provides a comprehensive list of books, websites, and other resources for further exploration of astrology and cannabis. Whether you are a beginner or an advanced practitioner, these resources will deepen your understanding and enhance your journey.

Books on Astrology

1. **"The Only Astrology Book You'll Ever Need" by Joanna Martine Woolfolk**
   - A comprehensive guide to astrology, covering everything from the basics to advanced interpretations. It includes detailed information on planetary positions, houses, and aspects.
2. **"Astrology for the Soul" by Jan Spiller**
   - This book focuses on the significance of the North Node in astrology, offering insights into your life's purpose and spiritual growth.
3. **"Parker's Astrology: The Definitive Guide to Using Astrology in Every Aspect of Your Life" by Julia and Derek Parker**
   - A detailed and visually rich guide to astrology that covers natal charts, transits, and more, suitable for all levels of interest.
4. **"Astrology: Using the Wisdom of the Stars in Your Everyday Life" by Carole Taylor**
   - A practical and accessible guide to astrology, including how to create and interpret your birth chart and understand the influence of the planets.

5. **"The Astrology of You and Me: How to Understand and Improve Every Relationship in Your Life" by Gary Goldschneider**
    - This book offers insights into how astrology influences your relationships, with practical advice for navigating different zodiac sign interactions.

Books on Cannabis

1. **"The Cannabis Encyclopedia: The Definitive Guide to Cultivation & Consumption of Medical Marijuana" by Jorge Cervantes**
    - An extensive guide covering all aspects of cannabis cultivation and use, including detailed strain information and medical applications.
2. **"Cannabis Pharmacy: The Practical Guide to Medical Marijuana" by Michael Backes**
    - A comprehensive resource on the medical use of cannabis, including information on strains, conditions, and dosing.
3. **"The Cannabis Manifesto: A New Paradigm for Wellness" by Steve DeAngelo**
    - A thought-provoking book that explores the benefits of cannabis and advocates for its acceptance and use as a wellness tool.
4. **"Marijuana Horticulture: The Indoor/Outdoor Medical Grower's Bible" by Jorge Cervantes**
    - A classic guide to cannabis cultivation, suitable for both beginners and experienced growers.
5. **"The Leafly Guide to Cannabis: A Handbook for the Modern Consumer" by The Leafly Team**
    - A modern guide to cannabis that covers strain selection, consumption methods, and the science behind cannabis effects.

Websites and Online Resources

1. **Astro.com**
   - A comprehensive astrology website offering free birth chart calculations, detailed horoscopes, and extensive astrological resources.
   - Astro.com

2. **Cafe Astrology**
   - A popular site for astrological reports, articles, and insights. Offers free birth chart interpretations and daily horoscopes.
   - Cafe Astrology

3. **The Astrology Podcast**
   - A podcast featuring discussions on various astrological topics, interviews with astrologers, and in-depth analyses of astrological events.
   - The Astrology Podcast

4. **Leafly**
   - An extensive resource for information on cannabis strains, effects, and user reviews. Includes educational articles and news about the cannabis industry.
   - Leafly

5. **NORML (National Organization for the Reform of Marijuana Laws)**
   - A non-profit organization focused on marijuana law reform and education. Provides information on cannabis legalization and advocacy.
   - NORML

6. **Project CBD**
   - A resource dedicated to promoting and publicizing research on the medical uses of cannabidiol (CBD) and other components of the cannabis plant.
   - Project CBD

Online Courses and Communities

1. **Astrology University**
   - Offers online courses and webinars on various astrological topics, taught by experienced astrologers.
   - Astrology University
2. **The Astrology School**
   - Provides online astrology courses and resources, including a comprehensive program for aspiring professional astrologers.
   - The Astrology School
3. **Growers Network**
   - An online community and resource hub for cannabis cultivators, offering forums, educational articles, and industry news.
   - Growers Network
4. **Cannabis Training University**
   - Offers comprehensive online courses on cannabis cultivation, medical applications, and the cannabis industry.
   - Cannabis Training University
5. **Astrology Weekly Forum**
   - A community forum for discussing all aspects of astrology, from beginner questions to advanced techniques.
   - Astrology Weekly Forum

Apps for Astrology and Cannabis

1. **TimePassages (Astrology)**
   - An astrology app offering detailed birth chart interpretations, daily horoscopes, and insights into planetary transits.
   - Available on iOS and Android.
2. **Co–Star Personalized Astrology (Astrology)**

- An AI-powered astrology app that provides personalized daily horoscopes and insights based on your birth chart.
- Available on iOS and Android.

3. **Leafly (Cannabis)**
   - A cannabis app that helps you explore strains, read user reviews, and find nearby dispensaries.
   - Available on iOS and Android.

4. **Eaze (Cannabis)**
   - A cannabis delivery app that connects users with local dispensaries and delivers products to their doorsteps.
   - Available on iOS and Android.

5. **Astro Future (Astrology)**
   - An astrology app offering detailed birth chart analyses, synastry charts, and daily horoscopes.
   - Available on iOS and Android.

These recommended readings and resources will provide you with a wealth of information and tools to deepen your understanding of astrology and cannabis. By exploring these books, websites, and communities, you can continue to expand your knowledge and enhance your practice, aligning your life with the natural rhythms of the cosmos and the healing potential of cannabis.

Appendix D: Strain Index by Astrological Sign

This appendix provides a quick reference guide matching specific cannabis strains to each zodiac sign. The recommended strains are chosen based on the unique traits, needs, and characteristics of each sign, helping to enhance their natural strengths and balance their challenges.

Aries: The Pioneer

Traits: Bold, energetic, adventurous, impulsive

Recommended Strains:

- **Jack Herer:** Enhances creativity and focus, perfect for Aries' dynamic and pioneering spirit.
- **Girl Scout Cookies:** Provides a balanced high, supporting Aries' need for both energy and relaxation.

Taurus: The Builder

Traits: Practical, reliable, patient, stubborn

Recommended Strains:

- **Granddaddy Purple:** Offers deep relaxation, helping Taurus unwind after hard work.
- **Northern Lights:** Provides a calming effect, supporting Taurus' need for stability and peace.

Gemini: The Communicator

Traits: Curious, adaptable, social, scattered

Recommended Strains:

- **Harlequin:** Enhances mental clarity and focus, perfect for Gemini's quick-thinking nature.

- **Lemon Haze:** Energizes and uplifts, supporting Gemini's social and communicative tendencies.

Cancer: The Nurturer
Traits: Emotional, nurturing, protective, sensitive
Recommended Strains:

- **Blue Dream:** Provides a balanced high, promoting emotional well-being and relaxation.
- **OG Kush:** Offers deep relaxation and stress relief, perfect for Cancer's nurturing nature.

Leo: The Leader
Traits: Confident, creative, charismatic, egotistical
Recommended Strains:

- **Pineapple Express:** Enhances creativity and energy, supporting Leo's vibrant and expressive personality.
- **Sour Diesel:** Provides an uplifting and energizing effect, perfect for Leo's leadership qualities.

Virgo: The Analyst
Traits: Analytical, practical, detail-oriented, critical
Recommended Strains:

- **ACDC:** Offers a clear-headed high, enhancing focus and reducing anxiety, ideal for Virgo's analytical mind.
- **Harlequin:** Promotes mental clarity and calmness, supporting Virgo's need for precision and order.

Libra: The Harmonizer
Traits: Diplomatic, balanced, social, indecisive
Recommended Strains:

- **Cherry Pie:** Enhances relaxation and social interaction, supporting Libra's harmonious nature.
- **Strawberry Cough:** Uplifts and energizes, perfect for Libra's social and balanced personality.

Scorpio: The Transformer

Traits: Intense, passionate, resourceful, secretive

Recommended Strains:

- **Trainwreck:** Provides a transformative and energizing high, supporting Scorpio's intense nature.
- **Gorilla Glue:** Offers deep relaxation and emotional release, perfect for Scorpio's need for intensity and depth.

Sagittarius: The Explorer

Traits: Adventurous, optimistic, philosophical, restless

Recommended Strains:

- **Super Lemon Haze:** Enhances energy and creativity, supporting Sagittarius' adventurous spirit.
- **Blue Dream:** Provides a balanced high, promoting relaxation and mental clarity, perfect for Sagittarius' explorative nature.

Capricorn: The Strategist

Traits: Ambitious, disciplined, responsible, pessimistic

Recommended Strains:

- **OG Kush:** Offers deep relaxation and stress relief, supporting Capricorn's need for balance and relaxation.
- **Bubba Kush:** Promotes calmness and focus, ideal for Capricorn's disciplined and strategic approach.

Aquarius: The Visionary

Traits: Innovative, independent, humanitarian, detached
Recommended Strains:

- **Sour Tangie:** Enhances creativity and innovation, supporting Aquarius' visionary ideas.
- **Pineapple Express:** Provides an uplifting and energizing effect, perfect for Aquarius' social and independent nature.

Pisces: The Dreamer
Traits: Compassionate, intuitive, artistic, escapist
Recommended Strains:

- **Purple Kush:** Offers deep relaxation and emotional release, supporting Pisces' need for introspection and calm.
- **Lavender:** Promotes tranquility and spiritual connection, perfect for Pisces' dreamy and compassionate nature.

Conclusion

This strain index provides a quick reference guide to help each zodiac sign select cannabis strains that complement their unique traits and needs. By choosing strains that align with your astrological sign, you can enhance your natural strengths, find balance, and navigate life's challenges with greater ease and well-being. Use this guide as a starting point for exploring the synergistic relationship between astrology and cannabis, and tailor your choices to suit your individual experiences and preferences.

Message from the Author:

I hope you enjoyed this book; I love astrology and knew there was not a book such as this out on the shelf. I love metaphysical items as well. Please check out my other books:

-Life of Government Benefits

-My life of Hell

-My life with Hydrocephalus

-Red Sky

-World Domination:Woman's rule

-World Domination:Woman's Rule 2: The War

-Life and Banishment of Apophis: book 1

-The Kidney Friendly Diet

-The Ultimate Hemp Cookbook

-Creating a Dispensary(legally)

-Cleanliness throughout life: the importance of showering from childhood to adulthood.

-Strong Roots: The Risks of Overcoddling children

-Hemp Horoscopes: Cosmic Insights and Earthly Healing

- Celestial Hemp Navigating the Zodiac: Through the Green Cosmos

-Astrological Hemp: Aligning The Stars with Earth's Ancient Herb

-The Astrological Guide to Hemp: Stars, Signs, and Sacred Leaves

-Green Growth: Innovative Marketing Strategies for your Hemp Products and Dispensary

-Cosmic Cannabis

-Astrological Munchies

-Henry The Hemp

-Zodiacal Roots: The Astrological Soul Of Hemp

- **Green Constellations: Intersection of Hemp and Zodiac**

-Hemp in The Houses: An astrological Adventure Through The Cannabis Galaxy

-Galactic Ganja Guide

Heavenly Hemp

Zodiac Leaves

Doctor Who Astrology

Cannastrology

Stellar Satvias and Cosmic Indicas

Celestial Cannabis: A Zodiac Journey

AstroHerbology: The Sky and The Soil: Volume 1

AstroHerbology:Celestial Cannabis:Volume 2

Cosmic Cannabis Cultivation

The Starry Guide to Herbal Harmony: Volume 1

The Starry Guide to Herbal Harmony: Cannabis Universe: Volume 2

Yugioh Astrology: Astrological Guide to Deck, Duels and more

Nightmare Mansion: Echoes of The Abyss

Nightmare Mansion 2: Legacy of Shadows

Nightmare Mansion 3: Shadows of the Forgotten

Nightmare Mansion 4: Echoes of the Damned

The Life and Banishment of Apophis: Book 2

Nightmare Mansion: Halls of Despair

Healing with Herb: Cannabis and Hydrocephalus

Planetary Pot: Aligning with Astrological Herbs: Volume 1

Fast Track to Freedom: 30 Days to Financial Independence Using AI, Assets, and Agile Hustles

Cosmic Hemp Pathways

How to Become Financially Free in 30 Days: 10,000 Paths to Prosperity

Zodiacal Herbage: Astrological Insights: Volume 1

Nightmare Mansion: Whispers in the Walls

The Daleks Invade Atlantis

Henry the hemp and Hydrocephalus

10X The Kidney Friendly Diet

Cannabis Universe: Adult coloring book

Hemp Astrology: The Healing Power of the Stars

Check out my Virtual dispensary for all your hemp needs: https://shift.store/sg1fan23477/retail

If you want solar for your home go here: https://www.harborsolar.live/apophisenterprises/

Get some shirts: https://www.bonfire.com/store/apophis-shirt-emporium/

Instagrams:

@apophis_enterprises,

@hempkingdom2024,

@apophisbookemporium,

@apophisfashion,

@apophisscardshop

Twitter: @apophisenterpr1,

Tiktok:@apophisenterprise

Youtube: @sg1fan23477

Podcast:Apophis Chat Zone: https://open.spotify.com/show/5zXbrCLEV2xzCp8ybrfHsk?si=fb4d4fdbdce44dec

Newsletter: https://apophiss-newsletter-27c897.beehiiv.com/

www.ingramcontent.com/pod-product-compliance
Lightning Source LLC
Chambersburg PA
CBHW050501160726

48003CB00001B/101